DISNEY

like a

BY RICK NAMEY

Fodor's Travel Publications, Inc.

New York • Toronto • London • Sydney • Auckland

http://www.fodors.com/

Disney Like a Pro

Editor: Karen Cure

Contributors: Rita Aero, Janet Atkins, Susan Blake, Howard and Donald Bradfute, Janet Tucker Butler, Audra Epstein, Ken Jones, Charles Namey, Ricky Namey, Terrie Namey, Tiffany Namey, Linda K. Schmidt, Donald Schutz

Creative Director: Fabrizio La Rocca

Cover and Text Design: Allison Saltzman

Cover Illustration: Steven Guarnaccia

Special Sales

Fodor's Travel Publications are available at special discounts for bulk purchases for sales promotions or premiums. Special editions, including personalized covers, excerpts of existing guides, and corporate imprints, can be created in large quantities for special needs. For more information, contact your local bookseller or write to Special Markets, Fodor's Travel Publications, 201 East 50th Street, New York, NY 10022. Inquiries from Canada should be directed to your local Canadian bookseller or sent to Random House of Canada, Ltd., Marketing Department, 1265 Aerowood Drive, Mississauga, Ontario L4W 1B9. Inquiries from the United Kingdom should be sent to Fodor's Travel Publications, 20 Vauxhall Bridge Road, London SW1V 2SA, England.

Important Advice

You can use this book in the confidence that all prices and opening times are based on information supplied to us at press time; Fodor's cannot accept responsibility for any errors. Time inevitably brings changes, so always confirm information when it matters.

Acknowledgments

Bonnie Ammer, Karen Cure, Allison Saltzman, and Audra Epstein at Fodor's; Tom Schroeder at Universal Studios; Craig Dezern at Walt Disney World; my mom and my brother, Charles Namey; Janet Atkins; Ken Jones, Dr. Zendell, and Don Schutz; special thanks to Gil Nogalski, Bob Kaplus, Hillie Meyers, and Neil Meyers; Robert Stricker, the world's greatest agent; and, most of all, Rita Aero. It would take another lifetime to thank her enough.

PRINTED IN THE UNITED STATES OF AMERICA
10 9 8 7 6 5 4 3 2 1

contents

dear reader

Since childhood, I have believed that "when you wish upon a star, your dreams come true." Growing up in Baltimore, distant Disneyland was an impossible dream. So I simply wished the Magic Kingdom to come to me. My wish required the Russians to launch Sputnik, thereby necessitating the transfer of most of America's rocket engineers (including my father) to an unknown town in the middle of Florida. Then, in the mid-1960s, I asked my waterskiing buddy Craig Linton, whose dad was in real estate, "Hey Craig, why don't you get your dad to sell 30,000 acres of orange grove to Walt Disney to build a theme park so we could all go to it?" The rest is history.

Obviously, the person who originally wished Walt Disney all the way from Anaheim to Orlando is the person most qualified to show you around. You will also get three genuine natives at no additional charge: my wife, Terrie; 13-year-old Tiffany; and nine-year-old Ricky, who has not missed a single season at Walt Disney World in his entire life. This is, and always has been, a family effort. Our goal is to help you and your family benefit from the knowledge that has taken us many years to acquire. We've tried our best to be accurate and complete (omitting only attractions we don't like and changeable details you can easily get elsewhere). Our wish is that our work makes *your* dreams come true.

—*Rick Namey*
Orlando, Florida

chapter 1

GRAB THE MOUSE BY THE TAIL!

The average room rate in Central Florida is under $50. A soda in a Disney theme park costs around $2. If each person in a family of four has a soft drink with lunch and dinner and takes three cold drink breaks—a reasonable proposition under the Florida sun—they'll spend $40 a day on sodas. It follows that for many visitors, the daily cost of the family's sodas is equal to the cost of its nightly lodging. And a full week of sodas costs the same as discount round-trip airfare to Orlando from many major cities.

Walt Disney World's press kit says that the Magic Kingdom serves more than 46 million Coca-Colas each year. Yet the figure includes only Coca-Colas, and not any other beverages. Yet in all of the years I've been going to the theme parks, never once have I heard anyone say that the highlight of his or her vacation was the fabulous cola in the parks.

I'm not saying that you should go without cold drinks on hot days. But as you read this book you will learn that there are a lot better things to do with your money in theme parks than buy cola.

I wrote this book to teach you things that only a person who's been here since they opened the place would know. To help you save money. And to show you how to save time. Because, ultimately, when you're on vacation, time is also money.

I suggest you start planning your trip by reading this book from cover to cover, as you would a good novel. Then make a tentative itinerary and estimate your costs as I explain below. With those numbers in hand, making almost every other decision about your vacation will be a lot easier.

FIGURE THE HOURLY COST OF YOUR VACATION

Let me explain. To understand the real cost of your visit to each Central Florida attraction, you also have to prorate what you spent to get to the area and stay there. The real cost of riding, say, Space Mountain involves your transportation, lodging, meals, and multi-day admission during your entire trip. And you can prorate this figure to give you an idea of how much each waking hour you spend in Orlando actually costs. The hourly figure, together with my exclusive one- to five-point Worth-It Ratings, which I give for every attraction in this book, provide a great answer to the question that arises each time you start a new activity or step into a long line: Is my experience going to be worth my time and my money?

To answer that question, you need to understand how much it's costing you just to be in Orlando on your theme-park vacation—and you need to break it down by the waking hour. Here's how to figure the hourly cost.

Transportation: Start with these expenses. Figure the family's airfare, airport transportation at both ends, parking, and/or car rental. If you drive to Orlando, allow for fuel, lodging and meals en route, and around 25 cents per mile for wear and tear on your car. Add the cost of transportation around Orlando, including bus fares or tour fees.

Food: Give yourself a daily budget that reflects meals you expect to have. In Orlando, a meal in a moderately priced restaurant might cost $20 to $30, excluding drinks, service, and tax; $30 to $40 in an expensive restaurant; and over $40 in a very expensive restaurant. In the theme parks, restaurants with table service are usually moderately priced. To be perfectly accurate about your vacation costs, subtract your normal grocery budget for the period from your estimated vacation expenditure (after all, you'd have to eat anyway).

Lodging: Add the cost of your hotel. Be sure to include tax and allow for phone and incidentals.

Tickets and Souvenirs: You know about the tickets. The souvenirs are inevitable, too. To keep these costs down, give each family member an allowance.

To get your estimated total vacation cost, add all these figures. Multiply the number of days you plan to be in Orlando by 12 (about how many hours most people tolerate in a theme park at a time). Then divide your total cost by total hours.

Let's look at how this works for a hypothetical New Jersey family planning a week in Orlando: Rick, Terrie, 12-year-old Tiffany, and 9-year-old Ricky Jones.

The round-trip Newark–Orlando flight costs $230 per person, $920 for the family. In New Jersey, they spend $30 for airport transportation each way. In Orlando, they rent a mid-size car for a flat $150. Add $10 a day for gas for a total of $80.

FIGURE THE HOURLY COST OF YOUR VACATION

They plan to eat mostly at inexpensive family restaurants, and they've allowed $960 for food, $560 more than they spend at home.

Lodging costs $52 a night. They budget $50 for movies and other incidentals at their hotel.

They plan to visit the Magic Kingdom, Epcot, and Universal. So they're buying two single-day, single-park Disney passes at $40.81 per day for each family member over 12 and $32.86 for Ricky. They get the five-day joint pass to Universal, Sea World, and Wet 'n' Wild for $95.35 each ($77.33 for Ricky). With one day left, they're heading for the Kennedy Space Center for $12 a head ($7 for Ricky). At each park, each person gets $10 in spending money; the family's total shopping allowance is $320.

Here's a recap of their budget:

Airfare and airport transport	$980
Rental car and gas	$230
Vacation food	$560
Hotel	$414
Magic Kingdom and Epcot passes	$311
Universal, Sea World, Wet 'n' Wild passes	$364
Kennedy Space Center	$43
Shopping	$320
Total	$3,222

With eight days in Orlando (at 12 hours per day), the Joneses have a total of 96 waking hours during their vacation. Dividing the $3,222 by 96 yields the hourly cost of the Jones family's vacation: $33.57.

Substitute your own figures. Then, when it looks like you're going to have to wait an hour to ride Dumbo, you won't just ask yourself if you want to take the time to ride. You'll also, inevitably, ask yourself whether you really feel that a ride on Dumbo is *really* worth $33.57.

GO WHERE YOU WANT TO GO,
DO WHAT YOU WANT TO DO!

Central Florida has no fewer than 11 theme parks. There are also seven water parks, over a dozen dinner shows, and several ticketed nightclub attractions. One of the reasons I wanted to write this book is that I've seen over and over that many people miss some of the best of them. When I was at Visitor Information Television and later at Visitor Information Radio, people constantly told us that the Kennedy Space Center was one of the top three places they wanted to visit. Yet surveys of what people actually visited always showed the Kennedy Space Center below that. What happened? Why did so many people who wanted to go to the Space Center travel all the way to Central Florida, then miss it?

Part of the answer is probably the simple fact that after most families go to Walt Disney World and its theme parks, they have neither time nor money left over. That's why I recommend an alternative strategy for your Central Florida vacation.

DO IT BACKWARDS Most people visit Disney first, and Disney does a really great job of taking advantage of that fact to keep them there—spending their money before they have a chance to spend it anywhere else. So by all means, figure out what you want to do in Orlando. And do it all. But if it includes destinations outside WDW, save the Mouse for last so that *you* see what *you* want.

I encourage you to begin your vacation at the park I consider the best park in the world: Universal Studios Florida (Universal for short).

MINIMIZE YOUR MOUSE We all know that Walt Disney World is the magnet that brings most people to Central Florida. However, some things at Walt Disney World are extremely expensive. And while some of them are not duplicated anywhere else in the world (and I tell you about the highlights in the chapters that follow), many things are available elsewhere—and at a lower cost.

Outside Walt Disney World, for instance, you can buy enough stuff with pictures of Mickey, Donald, Goofy, and the other Disney characters to last you a lifetime. Ditto for food, supplies, and other necessities, which cost significantly less at local discount stores.

GO WHEN YOU WANT TO GO Other guides make a lot of noise about the benefits of traveling off-season, when crowds are smaller and lines shorter. There are three problems with this theory.

First, it may not be possible to travel then. If your kids are in school, staying as long as you need to in order to see what you want means either missing school—or traveling when everyone else does.

Second, although lines may be shorter off-season, they may not move as quickly. Theme parks have the ability to open or close lines and add or subtract ride vehicles. This is not some conspiracy to cheat off-season guests. It's a way for parks to lower costs when there are fewer guests around.

Third, park hours are shorter off-season, so for any given length of vacation, the parks are available to you for fewer hours overall. Moreover, there may be fewer parades and shows. So, although you're paying less overall, your hourly cost may be more, and you're getting less.

My advice? Go when you want to go. The basic experience varies little from season to season. Don't be afraid of peak times, because the parks are geared up to provide a peak experience. And don't stay away from off-peak times, either. Room and travel rates are lower, compensating you for what you may be missing.

SAVE MONEY ON LODGINGS

GET THE LOWEST RATE If you're looking for a low rate on a room, you could go from hotel to hotel or stop at a pay phone and check around. But you still wouldn't know where the lowest rates are.

That's where room brokers come in. Try **Central Florida Tours** (tel. 800/396–1883), **Central Reservations Service** (tel. 800/873–4683), **Know Before You Go** (tel. 800/749–1993), or **Tourist Tips** (tel. 800/877–3137).

There is a standing rule in the hotel business that says, "An unsold room night is gone forever." Therefore, anything that a hotel can get out of a room is better than nothing. Room brokers purchase blocks of room nights from hotels; typically, they either commit to a high number of room nights in advance, or they pick up leftover rooms on a daily basis. Either way, they get incredibly low rates and pass the savings on to you. So a family of four can pay as little as $23 a night with no extra-person charges in a decent chain property. Or up to six can stay in a two-bedroom suite with a kitchen for an incredible $49 a night at a major chain hotel in the attractions area.

AVOID PHONE-RATE RIPOFFS During my years in the tourist industry, many hotels have told me that phone charges are their number-one source of extra revenue. At one large Orlando area hotel company that advertises especially low room rates, you have to leave a deposit at the front desk if you want a telephone, pay extra, and plug it in yourself. And then there was the very nice hotel on U.S. 192, a major visitor thorough-fare, where I used to book business associates at an unbeliev-ably low $32 a night. The catch was that the phone charges were outrageous. For business people who had to make a lot of calls, that $32 quickly became $100. When planning your trip to Orlando, be sure to consider your need for telephone when you book your lodging. Remember that you'll probably be call-ing locally a lot, to make reservations and get information. Even local charges add up. And just because the hotel uses AT&T, Sprint, or MCI doesn't mean you're protected: prices on calls for access to them can be horrendous. In advance, find out rates for local and long-distance calls (including those you make with your calling card or via Sprint, AT&T, or MCI). Then negotiate a better deal. And get it in writing.

SAVE BIG ON TICKETS
(OR GET THEM FREE)

NEVER PAY FULL PRICE Never buy theme-park tickets at the gate. That's generally the worst possible place to buy them. Not only will you pay more—you'll have to wait in line to do it. (And for our hypothetical family, the Joneses, just 10 min-utes in line costs them $5.56.) You'll find little booths with signs inviting you to ask about free or discount attraction tick-ets at convenience and souvenir stores, in parking lots, and in hotel lobbies as far north as Pedro's South of the Border, a hotel and attraction complex near Dillon, South Carolina. These booths are known in the trade as OPCs, short for Off-Premises Contractors. They really do sell discounted tickets, at between 10% and 20% off the walk-in price. For a family of four, that will amount to about $20 a day—$100 for a five-day vacation! Plus, you'll also save time standing in line.

NEGOTIATE WITH YOUR HOTEL FOR FREEBIES A travel agent may not get you the best deal on a hotel room, at least one in Orlando. For that, you have to deal with the hotel directly—preferably from home rather than while you're standing at the front desk, credit card in hand, with the kids just over your shoulder impatiently asking questions.

At chain hotels, which tend to have smaller staffs—Days Inns, Holiday Inns, and the like—ask for the manager, who is usually easily accessible. Say when you're coming and how long you plan to stay, and mention that you are comparing a number of properties to get the best deal. I usually say something like, "Sharpen your pencil, now. I'm going to be calling a lot of properties and comparing what they offer. If you want my business, I need your very best deal, now. Otherwise, if I get a better one down the street, you probably won't hear from me again." Actually, if they're at all competitive, they probably will hear from me again, because—and this is my favorite part—I always call them back to tell them my best deal and let them bid against it. Believe me, if you don't use a wholesale broker, you have to shop the hotels this way. Even if you call a couple of places, if you just take the rate they give you, you'll overpay.

When you negotiate, it helps to understand a little about the hotel business. One of the yardsticks by which hotel owners measure their managers and staffs is by the hotel's "average room rate," an average of what's taken in for all the hotel's room nights per night, per season, and per year. You probably already know that airfares vary widely; you can sit next to someone who paid half as much or even twice as much. That's also true of room rates. Because the management is so conscious of its average room rate, there is a rate beneath which they will not go. But the fact that your negotiations have brought you to this rate does not mean that the manager has nothing left to offer.

Most hotels have a stash of attraction tickets. Theme parks may have provided them as an incentive to send visitors there. The more people the employees send, the more free tickets they get. Other tickets may have been purchased from the theme parks, often at a discount, to resell to guests at a profit. If a manager really needs the room night, he or she may part with a few tickets.

Although you will seldom find these so-called comps at $18-a-night motels along U.S. 192, there are exceptions—particularly if you promise to stay a week or longer. In general, the closer the attraction, the more likely a hotel is to have comps to give away. For free Disney tickets, your best chance is at hotels on property in the Walt Disney World Village area and off property in the Lake Buena Vista area. For Universal, best odds are at motels on the north end of International Drive, another tourist main drag; for Sea World, if you're next door to the park on the south end of I-Drive (as International Drive is known around town). And so on.

Go for comps for water park and dinner shows first. They're easier to get, though the normal prices are similar to theme parks'. Basically, if you're going to pay for some of your tickets and get some free, it doesn't matter which are which.

Remember that the hotels get discounts, even on passes they buy. You should, too. So if you can't get comps (maybe because you got such a good deal on your room), try to buy tickets outright at a discount. Just say that you know that the hotel is selling tickets at a markup and that you want to buy tickets at the wholesale price as a condition of choosing that hotel.

If shuttle service to attractions is not included in your room rate, ask for a freebie when you negotiate over your room. Many hotels offer free shuttles to attractions, and usually some passengers have paid and some haven't. Don't be one of the losers. Mears, the area's largest shuttle operator (tel. 407/423–5566), charges about $10 per person for one round trip between any given hotel and any given theme park. For a family of four, that would be $40. A family's total outlay for lodging and transportation, when staying in a $40 room in a hotel without free shuttle service, would be comparable to the $80 they might pay for a room in a hotel that includes transportation. If you're not renting a car, a $69 room at the All-Star Resort, which is in Walt Disney World and includes all Disney transportation, will actually leave you with more money at the end of the day than a $30 a night room on U.S. 192 that doesn't include any transportation.

Just because you're driving your own car doesn't mean the shuttle has no value to you. Transportation is worth something. When you're negotiating for your best rate, tell the manager that you've spoken with Mears and that you know the value of the transportation and are factoring that into the equation when comparing various room rates. All other things being equal, a room that doesn't include transportation should not sell for the same rate as one that does.

Always keep in mind that Orlando has more hotel rooms than any other single locality on the entire planet. Though rates are extremely low and supply is very high, local developers keep building more. Except for a few peak weeks of the year, there is tremendous competition for your business. The hotels need you a lot more than you need them. If a hotel, including any of those on my list, acts like they don't want your business, move on! There are plenty more who do.

TOUR A TIME SHARE AND SAVE! When you buy a time share, as so-called interval-ownership resorts are informally known, you buy partial ownership of a condominium-type unit, which you are then allowed to use for a given length of time during the year, usually one week.

SAVE BIG ON TICKETS (OR GET THEM FREE)

Because time-share resorts offer some of Orlando's best accommodations, with excellent facilities, you may well *want* to tour a time share. But if you're really serious about saving money, there's another good reason to do so. Some big operators pay cash—sometimes $50 to $75—to people who agree to take a 90-minute tour. Most others offer free attraction tickets.

To find out about these, keep your eyes open for OPCs, described above, who contract with time-share resorts to deliver people who are willing to take the tours. If you ask about the free tickets (as opposed to discounted tickets), the OPC operator will tell you about time-share tours.

Know the rules: Don't be afraid to take the tour. A time-share tour can be a relatively painless way to get free tickets. Always remember that time-share promoters are required by law to abide by any offer they make. If the terms read "No purchase necessary," then you are under no obligation to buy anything.

Many developers give the OPCs budgets with which to buy tickets to give away as premiums—enough to give you tickets to a Disney park, Universal, or another major attraction. But because anything they don't spend is profit, they try to get away with giving you the least expensive premium possible. Insist on tickets to a major park. And walk away if you don't get them. If you settle for a vague promise like, "I'll see what I can do," chances are you'll end up with tickets to Ralph's Roach Ranch and Ball of String Museum.

The invitation to tour the property, which the OPC gives you when you agree to take the tour, spells out the rules of the game. Always get the premium offer in writing. If the OPC offers you two free tickets to Universal, the invitation should say "two free tickets to Universal Studios Florida." The invitation also details the qualifications you must meet. Generally, you must be married and traveling with your spouse, have at least $40,000 annual household income, live outside Florida, and be "creditworthy."

Always take the morning tour. This usually gets you free breakfast. It interferes least with your day. Remember that by law, the operator has to abide by his offer. If the offer mentions a 90-minute presentation, then 90 minutes are all you are obligated to give. When 90 minutes are up, you are free to go, and they must provide transportation.

Don't leave without your premium: When the tour ends, the salesperson completes and verifies your certificate. You then turn it in at the time share's redemption office and get your premium—in this case, your tickets.

You may actually want to buy a time share. That would be another chapter. But some advice in the meantime. Look for a property that has the facilities you want and good security—that's only sensible. Go for a larger property. It's the extras that will affect how easy your property is to exchange. Most larger time shares belong to an international network of properties and you can probably exchange your week for a week at another resort in the group. And the quality of the network's other properties has significant impact on your property's resale value. If you are considering a previously owned time share, make sure that it comes with the exchange privilege; sometimes it's not transferrable, so the resale is not the bargain it seems.

DON'T PAY TO PARK HOP! Many years ago, multi-day passes not only let you visit all the major Disney theme parks on any given day; they also offered significant savings over single-day, single-park tickets. Now you pay extra for a privilege that used to be included. It isn't a lot extra, and the pass is heavily promoted, and so to most visitors, it sounds like a good idea. (*See* pages 227–229 for detailed information.)

I disagree. In my experience, the Park Hopper feature has practically no value. That's because getting into a theme park takes time (and remember, time is very closely related to money). Getting into a theme park requires parking your car, waiting for a tram, riding it to the entrance, waiting in line there, and then walking from the entrance some distance past the shops and eateries to the attractions. Leaving is the same process in reverse. Traveling between parks means taking a tram, bus, boat, or shuttle, and more waiting. Not long ago, in the off season, I left the Disney–MGM Studios at 4:30 PM headed for Disney's Old Key West Resort, where my companion intended to freshen up before a 6:30 dinner in Pleasure Island. Although we moved as quickly as we could and spent only 15 minutes at the hotel, we were an hour late for dinner.

I simply can't recommend that you waste perfectly good ride-and-attraction time on the leaving-and-arriving routine. So I advise you against park-hopping. And I certainly don't recommend that you pay extra to do it.

STICK WITH ONE-DAY, ONE-PARK DISNEY TICKETS Disney makes a big deal out of the fact that multi-day passes, which cost somewhat less per day than one-day, one-park tickets, are good forever. They are. However, by state law (which says a lot about Florida politics), theme park passes can't be transferred or sold. So if you live far from Orlando and never get back, the extra days may turn out to be worthless to you—and you wouldn't even be able to give them away to your friends. (The Four-Day Value Pass costs $136.74 or $34.19 a day, just $6.62 a day less than the $40.81 cost of a single-day theme park ticket. If your plans change and you use the pass for only three days, the prorated per-day cost is $45.58, nearly $5 a day more than the cost of a single ticket.) Buying one-day, one-park tickets buys you flexibility. Regardless of the number of days, Disney tickets admit you to three parks: the Magic Kingdom,

Epcot, and Disney–MGM Studios, one of the area's two movie-theme parks. The better of the pair (*and* the best theme park of all) is Universal Studios Florida. Since multiday Disney tickets cost almost the same per day as single tickets, I recommend one-day, one-park tickets to Disney's one-of-a-kind parks; spend the rest of your ticket budget on Central Florida tourism's best-ever deal, the five-day $89 pass that admits you to Universal, Sea World, *and* Wet 'n' Wild—which works out to an absolutely unheard-of $17.80 a day. This is a spectacular value, so inexpensive that even if you use the pass for only three days, your cost per day is still under $30, way less than the $38.50 tab for a single-day ticket to Universal.

SAVE MONEY ON INCIDENTALS

BYO DRINKS If you really want to save money, one excellent place to cut back is on sodas. It absolutely galls me to pay $2 for a cola when a juice box that's easy to tote in my backpack or stash in a locker costs between a quarter and fifty cents. (I'll tell you more about the great lockers below.) And, as I said, I have yet to run into a family whose best memory of the parks was their soft drinks.

BYO FOOD The more you feed yourself, the more you can save. Theme-park fast food for four costs between $20 and $30 per meal; packing sandwiches can trim $40 to $50 a day off your budget. And no one ever seems to mind when we brown-bag it.

USE SHOPPING PASSES If there's something you must have that's only available inside one of the Disney theme parks, don't pay another admission: You can get a complimentary, limited-time shopping pass, a really nice feature made for us locals. Go to Guest Relations, ask for a shopping pass, tell them what you want to buy, and pay for a one-day admission. If you convince them you don't have the time to go elsewhere, they'll give you about an hour. Return to Guest Relations within the specified time, show your purchases, and claim a refund.

DON'T WASTE TIME GETTING AROUND

LEAVE THE DRIVING TO SOMEONE ELSE Don't be too quick to rent a car. Surprisingly, you can get just about anywhere, even the Space Center, more easily on a shuttle. Buses to WDW, whether run by Disney or not, get you closer to the parks' entrance turnstiles and get you in and out of the park area with a lot less hassle. The same is true at other parks. You'll really appreciate the convenience at the end of the day, when the last thing you feel like doing is to wait in another line just to get to your car. The cost can be advantageous, too, providing you've struck a favorable deal on your lodgings.

ALWAYS KNOW WHERE YOU ARE GOING Get good directions (and a good map) at your hotel or the airport, and use them. Bad directions can get you in trouble. Church Street Station, for example, borders a part of town where you really don't want to be lost—trust me.

Central Florida directions can be very confusing. Interstate 4, which is marked east and west (because it's an east–west highway, running between Daytona and Tampa), actually runs north and south through Orlando. When you're thinking about I–4, just remember that east is actually north, and west is really south.

Don't make the mistake that many visitors do of confusing I–4 with the area's other "I," I-Drive, the nickname for International Drive. U.S. 192, the main attractions strip in the Magic Kingdom area, also goes by too many names. In addresses in this book we use its long formal name, the Irlo Bronson Memorial Highway. It's also called Space Coast Parkway; in downtown Kissimmee, it's Vine Street. U.S. 441 is also known as Orange Blossom Trail. There's not much here unless you're into XXX movies, except for the Florida Mall (*see* Chapter 12). Don't go without dependable transportation, good directions, and plenty of gas.

BEAT THE LINES

I once saw a comedian on *The Tonight Show* who began his stand-up act with the lines, "I just got back from Orlando. I'd like to do my impression of a day at Disney World." Then, he walked up and down the stage in small square patterns, simulating the maze-like path of a line at a theme park. The audience howled, then applauded. Everyone recognized a shared and despised experience.

Believe it or not, the parks are full of short cuts, short lines, off-peak times at attractions and restaurants, and many other opportunities to save time. Think like a football player and look for the openings. Keep your eyes peeled and keep re-prioritizing your schedule. Yes, it's a good idea to have a plan. But you need to keep yourself open to the timesaving opportunities that are always popping up along the way. The minutes you save with my strategies will add up to extra rides.

I'm not going to promise you freedom from lines. Unfortunately, they're part of the deal. I *can* promise that if you follow my advice, the lines you do wait in will be shorter and fewer.

PARK SMART As I've said before, just arriving at one of the Disney theme parks offers several opportunities to wait in line; leaving, you do the whole thing in reverse, minus the wait at the ticket windows. However, while people who come to the theme parks usually straggle in throughout the day, most visitors leave at closing time. That's when you find the worst lines of the day, when everyone's tired. That's why I devised my system of parking at the hotels.

For the Magic Kingdom: With my system here, I skip the lines to park, I skip the wait for the tram to the main gate, and I skip the lines waiting for Magic Kingdom transportation. It's even better at the end of the day.

As I approach the toll booth at the main entrance, I get into the lane furthest to the right. I pay the parking fee and keep to the right. When I see signs pointing to the hotels, I go either to the Polynesian Village Resort or the Contemporary Resort Hotel.

From the Poly (that's what the insiders call it), I turn in at the first entrance, stay to the right, and go to the last lot. This puts me next to the walkway into the Magic Kingdom. Then, I just walk down the path to the TTC. Sometimes, during peak seasons, in the entrance lane to the Polynesian's parking lot, an attendant asks to see my hotel ID. I answer that I'm having breakfast in the hotel. In over 20 years, at least 100 times, this system has failed only twice, on some of the busiest days on record. The attendant who turned me back told me that only registered guests could park at the hotel. He told me that in order to have breakfast there I should park in the main lot and take the bus to the Poly from the TTC. This left me in exactly the same position that I would have been in had I not tried.

At the Contemporary, I park as close to Space Mountain as possible since the walkway from the hotel to the Magic Kingdom is nearby. On the occasions that I was challenged and didn't get through, I went into the hotel and up to the Grand Canyon Concourse to catch the monorail, which stops right in the hotel. It's almost never crowded and takes me right into the park.

To Epcot and Disney–MGM Studios: Our new route for these is to park at Disney's BoardWalk (just follow the Epcot Resorts signs to Epcot Resorts Boulevard) and take the boats to the parks. We haven't had any trouble; Disney seems to want to encourage people to visit BoardWalk, which is a really neat place. Parking is free and so is the boat, which takes you directly to the parks.

ARRIVE LATE AND LEAVE LATE Most people take an unrealistic view of how long they'll spend in a park. During peak seasons, when hours are extended, they may arrive at 9 AM and expect to leave at midnight. Some visitors even attempt this endurance contest with children. Few make it. As a result, crowds thin considerably around dark. That's why I always advise my friends to sleep in (or attend a free time-share breakfast and pick up free theme park tickets). Relaxed and rested, they'll arrive late. They'll start at the front of the park, where lines have abated, and stay late enough to see the fireworks. They then have the park practically to themselves, along with a few thousand parkwise visitors.

BE CONTRARY Most people are creatures of habit, engaging in predictable behavior at predictable times. In theme parks, most visitors arrive between 9 and 10 AM. They eat lunch between 11 AM and 1:30 PM. They have dinner between 4 and 7 PM. Waits for all rides are shorter around lunch—and there are almost no lines for food between 2 and 3 PM.

While in the park, my advice is the same: Be contrary. If you arrive early, head for the back of the park first. Most people start at the front. If you arrive after the park has been open for at least an hour, start at the front.

And remember that you can save a couple of hours a day eating at off-peak times. My family usually has lunch at about 2 PM.

Decide which attractions you want to visit most and do them in REVERSE order. Most people have the same favorites. As the day goes on the most popular rides become less crowded. If you visit them in reverse order, you'll see more and spend less time standing in lines. Lines for some popular attractions almost never thin out, particularly when they're still relatively new. My suggestion is to line up when your tour through the park brings you to them. Then bite the bullet and wait.

The parades and fireworks at the theme parks are spectacular. But remember, you can't do everything and life is full of trade-offs. Lines are shortest during the parades and fireworks (and, during parades, particularly at the rides and shows nearest the parade route). Parades are usually late in the day, in the afternoon and at night. Decide what's more important—to see the parade or to catch that major ride. (Our hypothetical Jones family might ask themselves how they'd be happier spending $33.57 per hour.)

KEEP LEFT AND DON'T FOLLOW THE CROWD Most people follow the crowd, any crowd. Crowds usually flow to the right. Most people in a hurry pass on the left. If you make it a practice to stay left, you will usually be in the shortest and fastest lines. Also, many attractions run two lines. Because people follow each other and because the crowd moves right, there is often no line at all on the left. It's a Catch-22—no

one is in the left line because no one is in the left line to follow. I've seen park attendants walk way out into a long line
and remind people that there is another line open. Even on
peak days, I have often entered rides with no lines at all, just
by walking up the left lane—while hundreds waited patient-
ly on the right.

The last time we were at the Magic Kingdom, the line at
Big Thunder Mountain stretched all the way down the hill.
Looking up at the entrance, I noticed that the left lane was
open. My family and I ran up to it, all the way to the entrance,
and walked right onto the ride. We entered ahead of hundreds
of people who had been waiting 45 minutes or more, simply
because we knew enough not to follow the crowd.

In the Haunted Mansion, the line suddenly moves into a
big open area that is a sort of a free-for-all, just before visitors
get into the little black ride vehicles. These are on the right.
So the crowd always pushes in that direction. This always
leave a large open space along the left wall. We walk through
this space—right to the head of the line. It works every time.

Remember, wherever ropes mark off different queues, a
line that's closed will always be indicated by a chain across the
opening. If you see no chain, walk on in!

DON'T LINE UP WHEN THERE'S NO LINE Many rides and
shows have lobby areas or other collection spots where people are asked to wait. The expectation is that they'll wait in a
sort of orderly mob. However, most visitors form a line—out
of habit—leaving large open spaces empty. You can move
right in.

Look for the door and stand near it. If you can't see where
it is (because often these doors are disguised), ask the attendants: They'll always cheerfully tell you where you'll be going
next.

BE PARKWISE There are times that you'll find unusually short lines at even the most popular rides. Be parkwise: Don't bypass a short line to stick to a schedule.

PRAY FOR RAIN A typical summer day in Orlando starts out cloudy and gets progressively more so until mid- to late afternoon, when it rains for around an hour or two. That days like this come frequently—sometimes every day—sounds like bad news. But it's not.

Because these are ideal days to visit the theme parks. The cloudy weather scares many people away. Although some hardy souls brave the clouds, many more are flushed out by the rain. When the rain lets up, you may find the theme park practically to yourself.

So come prepared. We found rain ponchos for a dollar each at a discount store not long ago. You might want to buy a rain poncho with Mickey's picture on it (at about $5) or a nifty souvenir umbrella bearing the likeness of the Mickster, Woody Woodpecker, or Shamu. Since most of the lines are covered most of the time, find a long line you've been avoiding as soon as the rain starts. By the end of the ride, the shower may be over.

HAVE A GREAT TIME!

DRESS FOR THE WEATHER—AND FOR COMFORT Did you hear the one about the man who survived a fall from the Tower of Terror? He was wearing his light fall suit! Bad jokes notwithstanding, this is important. Always check the forecast before you leave for Orlando. Check again every day before you leave your hotel. And dress appropriately.

In winter, cold air masses from the north occasionally push southward, and temperatures drop. Thinking back on Christmases past, I can remember many in the 80s and many in the 30s or 40s. But once a cold front moves through, the weather instantly becomes tropical again. Many 40-degree days are followed by 80-degree days and vice versa. Sometimes cold nights follow warm days. Around Thanksgiving and between Christmas and New Year's, when the theme parks are open late, this is a consideration. Bring a jacket or even a change of clothes.

SHIP YOUR PURCHASES—DON'T CARRY THEM If you're staying at a WDW hotel, one of your many perks as a guest is free delivery of theme-park purchases to your room. Request it when you pay. And note that whether or not you're staying on property, you can have purchases shipped home or to anywhere in the world directly from the park. You pay only for the shipping—Disney does not tack on an extra charge for this service.

USE THE LOCKERS All parks have them, and I can't stress enough how helpful they can be. Putting your things in a convenient locked box can make your whole day better. Over the years, I have seen many thousands of miserable people, slogging around in the afternoon heat loaded down with gear and purchases.

While no one can guarantee the safety of your stuff and there certainly have been thefts and break-ins, I myself have never had a problem in over 20 years. And the lockers are a heck of a lot safer than the trunk of your car in the parking lot.

I use the locker for heavy, bulky things, like jackets, sweaters, and rain ponchos. You will want your cameras to record the day's events on film and video. But you will be miserable if you lug this equipment around all day. Use the locker (discreetly) to give yourself a break.

We also bring:

- A couple of towels to dry off with in case it rains.
- A change of socks for every member of the family. You'll be amazed how much a pair of dry socks can do for you after a rain or a hot, sweaty day.
- Frozen box drinks.
- Sandwiches and snacks.
- Extra film and video tape.

RIDE THE FRONT CAR While hundreds or thousands of visitors wait in line for a seat in one of the Disney monorails, my family and I are being personally escorted to the front of the train by a uniformed attendant to ride with the driver. I have overheard first-time visitors to Walt Disney World whisper "Who are they?" or "They must be V.I.P.s." There's a trick to this, and I can tell you what it is.

We ask. That's it. That's all. We just ask.

Disney's absolutely unadvertised policy is that anyone who asks can usually get a front seat. This is true on almost any ride—the monorail, Space Mountain, Big Thunder Mountain, Splash Mountain, Pirates of the Caribbean, even It's a Small World. You may have to wait until the next ride, or even the one after that, but if you want a front seat, they'll try to accommodate you. And the Disney panorama you see through the high-speed train's Plexiglas bubble is spectacular. As many times as we have done it, it's always a thrill.

USE SUNSCREEN This may seem obvious, but believe me, it's not. At the end of the day in the theme parks I see way too many sunburned noses. Remember that Florida sun will burn you even on overcast days and in winter. So put on sun block with a sun protection factor of 15 or higher—before you leave your motel, and bring extra. If you're going to a water park, be sure your sun block is waterproof and refresh it every few hours.

PREPARE TO GET WET In many parks (and not only the water parks), at least part of the fun is getting wet. You may want to bring a round of dry clothes for the family. And, because seeing your kids get wet makes for great pictures, I always bring a zip-closing plastic bag to put over my camera (I use a freezer-type bag over my video camera). Then I shoot right through the bag—a poor man's sports camera! If you're worried, bring one of those waterproof disposable cameras.

BEAT THE HEAT The Florida sun can wear you down. Next to staying inside where it's air-conditioned, the best way to beat the heat is to get wet. Our family cools off by spritzing each other frequently with a spray bottle loaded with water. We can be seen sticking our heads under the stream of water in the drinking fountains. Now and then, I step into the restroom, soak my T-shirt in the sink, and put it back on. It works! I'm cool for hours. (The one drawback: Tiff, my daughter, and Ricky, my son, don't think so.)

BE KIND TO YOUR KIDS All too frequently I overhear parents in the theme parks yelling at their children, even hitting them. Sometimes even the best children need a little discipline. That's not what I'm talking about. I'm talking about overbearing parents who are herding their children through the parks, determined to make them have a good time or else. Yes, there are ways to get through the parks faster, but don't overdo it! Don't try so hard to do so much that you miss the most important thing of all—a good time.

HAVE A GREAT TIME!

chapter 2

THE MAGIC KINGDOM

Walt Disney World

Take I–4 to Exit 25B, the Magic Kingdom/U.S. 192.

Worth-It Rating: 4
Add 1 if you have children under 10. Subtract 1 if you've been there before and seeing it again makes you skip another park that you've never visited.

When they think of Central Florida theme parks, most people think first of the Magic Kingdom. It was the first of the Florida Disney parks and is still the favorite of millions. Opened in October 1971 by Roy Disney, nearly five years after the death of his brother, Walt—whose dream it was and who acquired all the land—it has changed little in its more than a quarter of a century. It was patterned after California's Disneyland, the first true American theme park. But although the Magic Kingdom is similar to Disneyland, there are many differences. Disneyland occupies 80 acres, the Magic Kingdom over 100. Disneyland is surrounded by commercial businesses owned by others; of the 45 square miles that surround the Magic Kingdom, much of it is wilderness and all is owned by the Disney company.

While most of Disneyland's rides and attractions are also at WDW, they are not all in the Magic Kingdom. Star Tours, first built at Disneyland, is in Disney–MGM Studios theme park at Walt Disney World.

The Magic Kingdom's biggest drawback is its age. The concepts for many of its attractions were originally devised by Walt Disney in the 1940s, nearly 50 years ago. Audio-Animatronics, the computer-controlled system of hydraulics responsible for animating many of the robots you see in WDW, were dazzling in the mid-1950s, when they debuted. But they're almost nostalgia pieces now. For little kids, the Magic Kingdom is still the number one WOW!-inspiring place on this earth. For those of us with a little more life experience, it may seem dated.

TIMING I usually average an attraction every 45 minutes. But even if you hit two adventures an hour, you need more than two days here, even with extended hours.

EATERTAINMENT Because meals outside the theme parks cost about half as much as similar fare within the gates, our family tries not to eat in the parks. But we do love to eat. And sometimes we just can't help it. A couple of restaurants in the Magic Kingdom require reservations (noted below); to book a table, call 407/WDW–DINE.

PARADES AND PYROTECHNICS In addition to attractions, the Magic Kingdom has lots of street entertainment and a few sit-down shows. There are also several parades, which start in Town Square, head down Main Street, then meander through Frontierland; our favorite viewing spot is from the Mile Long Bar in Frontierland—you're right next to the parade route and you can sit, munch, and sip and still see it all. The brochure you get when buying your ticket comes with an entertainment schedule listing parade and show times. Or you can pick one up at City Hall or call 407/824–4321 for times in advance.

Daily Parade: The daily parade always features giant floats and costumed characters marching to Disney theme music. Even the least of these is better than any parade anywhere. The floats are dazzling, the characters are the ones you know and love, and the music jams. Whatever the theme, the time is daily at 3 PM, weather permitting. I rate it a 4 out of 5 points on my Worth-It scale.

Mickey's Very Merry Christmas Parade: Between Thanksgiving and New Year's, you'll see Mickey as Santa instead of the daily parade. I rate this a 5.

SpectroMagic: In this fabulous nighttime light parade, millions of lights adorn dozens of Disney characters and floats as they parade down Main Street. Outside peak seasons, you can see it as early as 6:15; in peak seasons, it runs at 8 and 10 or 9 and 11. I rate it a solid 5!

Fantasy in the Sky: A rousing soundtrack accompanies one of the world's largest and most dazzling fireworks displays, above the Cinderella Castle. In the early days of the park, this was just an occasional treat. I remember seeing coverage on the local news and going out to the park just for the fireworks. Over the years, it has become an increasingly important part of the daily schedule. You can see the show from virtually anywhere in the park. My most memorable viewpoints are all up high, especially from the top of the Astro-Orbiter (formerly Star Jets), the Monorail, and the Skyway (going in either direction). Whether or not you will be in the right place at just the right time is purely a matter of luck. Off season, the pyrotechnics start as early as 7; during holiday periods, that may be later.

SHOPPERTOONITIES If your schedule is really jam-packed, you may not have time to shop elsewhere. And some things are simply not available outside the gates. The highlight of many vacations is the photo of the family (in mouse ears) in front of Cinderella Castle. Don't blow the whole effect just to save the $5 a head on these hats.

THE LAY OF THE LAND In the Magic Kingdom, there are seven different lands with more than 50 attractions: Main Street USA leads from the entrance turnstiles and an area known as Town Square to the so-called Hub, in the shadow of the towering Cinderella Castle. Ranged around the Hub are all the other lands: Adventureland, Frontierland, Fantasyland, Mickey's Toontown Fair, Tomorrowland, and Liberty Square. Each has appropriately themed attractions, shows, eateries, and shops.

THE FAST TRACK In other parks, I advise you to travel clockwise. This is for the simple reason that most people are right handed and bear right wherever they go. My theory is to go the way other people don't. Because of the design of the Magic Kingdom, with the Cinderella Castle in the middle, many people head straight into Fantasyland. Others head left into Adventureland. The least conspicuous route is the walkway into Tomorrowland, and this is where I suggest you begin. Since you always want to start with a busy ride so that you miss the longest lines, head first for Space Mountain or Alien Encounter. Then tour the park counter-clockwise, ending in Adventureland.

Another favorite strategy of ours is to take the Walt Disney World Railroad straight to Toontown, then into Fantasyland, followed by Liberty Square, Frontierland, Adventureland, and Tomorrowland.

Choose what you want to see carefully. Wait times are posted on boards near the entrance to queue areas. In addition, message boards throughout the park give you scheduled entertainment and character appearances.

MAIN STREET USA

This old-fashioned street full of shops is mobbed right before and after parades and at the end of the day.

WALT DISNEY WORLD RAILROAD Real antiques dating from the turn of the century, these little engines pull you through most of the Kingdom, with stops at Main Street, Frontierland, and Mickey's Toontown Fair. In a way, this train planted the seed that became Disneyland and started the whole theme park concept: It was Walt's desire to expand the ride-on train he built for himself and his daughters at his home in California that inspired him to build Disneyland. Here, when there's not much of a line, the train is a quick way into the heart of the park. The ride is also a great place to videotape most of the park. You can shoot a quick movie of most of the park, stop at Mickey's Toontown Fair (the only place in the park where you're guaranteed a photo op with the reigning rodent), shoot the kids with Mickey, then come back to the station and drop your camera in a locker.
Worth-It Rating: 4

MAIN STREET CINEMA *Steamboat Willie,* the first Mickey Mouse cartoon and Disney's first talkie, is featured here in an old-time movie theater. After a 10-minute introductory film, the gang appears in selected shorts. How this little movie created the entire cartoon industry and made Walt Disney an eternal force in films simply fascinates me. My kids were bored.
Worth-It Rating: 2. Add 1 if you're a nostalgia buff.

MAIN STREET VEHICLES Several old-time vehicles, including a vintage fire engine and trolleys pulled by gigantic horses, take you one-way down Main Street.

Worth-It Rating: 3. Add 2 if there's no wait.

BITES Over the years one of the most common questions I've been asked about the Magic Kingdom is "What's in the Cinderella Castle?" The answer is **King Stefan's Banquet Hall.** There's standard steak and seafood at lunch and dinner and a breakfast with Disney characters in the morning—guests also get into the park early. Reserve ahead. **Tony's Town Square Restaurant** re-creates the site of one of the most romantic moments in motion picture history, the passionate spaghetti kiss in *Lady and the Tramp.* Naturally, the cuisine is Italian. The decor is the Italian cliché, with stained glass windows and ceiling fans. It's wonderful. Reservations are essential. At snack time, hit the **Main Street Bake Shop,** for famous Toll House cookies, or the **Plaza Ice Cream Parlor** for two scoops. I wish I could count the times I've stopped at **Casey's Corner** for a hot dog and Casey at the keyboard. It's right on the corner as you turn off Main Street towards Adventureland. At the **Plaza Restaurant,** at the Hub end of Main Street, the theme is turn-of-the-century and the food is deli style. Reservations are recommended. The **Crystal Palace,** probably the best dining deal in the park, serves an all-you-can-eat buffet with carved meats, hot vegetables, and a lavish fresh salad bar at lunch and dinner.

ENTERTAINMENT The **Dapper Dans,** Main Street's classic barbershop quartet—complete with straw hats—sing your favorites in tight harmonies. The brass-and-drum **Walt Disney World Marching Band** plays old-time and contemporary music. The **Rhythm Rascals** are an old fashioned rag-time band. Finally, below the Cinderella Castle, you'll often find the **Kids of the Kingdom** and other entertainers on the Magic Kingdom's main stage.

Worth-It Rating: 3. Add 1 if you like nostalgia, 1 more if you have lots of time.

SHOPPING This is really the biggest attraction on Main Street. Little stores line both sides of the road. One thing many people don't realize is that though they all look like individual storefronts on the outside (and inside have varying decor that makes them all look pretty different), they're actually contiguous. So on hot days, you can walk almost from one end of the street to the other in air-conditioned comfort by cutting through the stores. Here are a few shops that stand out.

The **Firehouse Gift Station** sells character toys and clothing with a firehouse theme. **Disneyana Collectibles** is where you can sign your name in the Magic Kingdom guest book. The shop features real and reproduced animation cells, figurines, and other Disney art and collectibles. The **Emporium** is the largest and most complete of the stores in the Magic Kingdom. Dominating Main Street at the Town Square end, it sells just about everything Disney.

Every Christmas, shop windows display spectacularly animated tableaux depicting Disney feature films. It takes me back to the days when I was a little kid and one of the highlights of the season was a visit to the wonderful animated windows at Macy's in New York.

Where to get your own monogrammed set of Mickey Mouse ears? The **Chapeau** is it! Only $5 plus tax, the hats used to be available only in basic black. Now, they come in a variety of colors and styles. Mine says "Annette" (really!). The **Main Street Camera Center,** the park's central camera store, stocks film, tapes, and accessories. They also sell and rent cameras, including video cams. **Uptown Jewelers,** the Tiffany's of the theme park, stocks a complete selection of

Disney jewelry. How about a gold Mickey Mouse watch? In the **Shadow Box,** silhouette artists snip portraits of your loved ones. You can watch glassblowers at work in **Crystal Arts.** Just keep a close rein on your littl'uns.

TOMORROWLAND

For the last few years I have felt that Tomorrowland was what we used to think the 1990s would be like back in the 1950s. In 1995, a redesigned Tomorrowland opened with several top-notch, brand-new attractions. It's the freshest and brightest spot in the Kingdom—and a great place to start. By the way, there's also an arcade.

THE TIMEKEEPER Robin Williams plays the robot emcee of this time-travel experience, which combines Disney's Circle-Vision 360 filming technique with Audio-Animatronics technology to create an adventure in which a typical family interacts with legendary sci-fi writers and time-travel experts Jules Verne and H. G. Wells. Well done! The special effects are brilliant!
Worth-It Rating: 5

ALIEN ENCOUNTER The story is about an interplanetary spacecraft that is foolishly transporting some dangerous alien life forms. Guess what? They get loose and slime you! Universal's Terminator 3D is a better execution of a similar concept. Still, this update of Mission to Mars is a real romp!
The Fast Track: Try to hit this attraction when the waiting room is about half full. All seats are good.
Worth-It Rating: 5

DREAMFLIGHT This one is not too high-tech but has nice visuals and a great sound track. Proving that every ride has its fans, this fairly simple little attraction is my wife Terrie's favorite Tomorrowland stop. You board a moving car that takes you through the history of commercial flight from barnstormers to jets. Big screens, wind machines, and tilting tracks create the feeling of flight. There's almost never a line and you can do the whole thing in a few minutes.
Worth-It Rating: 4

ASTRO ORBITER This is the old Star Jets ride, like Dumbo without the ears. Except here, you're extra high because the boarding area is one flight up, accessible via elevator. The high point is that it's a WDW high point—with a great view!
Worth-It Rating: 2. Add 3 if you can time your ride to catch the fireworks.

TOMORROWLAND TRANSIT AUTHORITY Once known as the PeopleMover, this little train on an electromagnetic track takes you through Tomorrowland and through Space Mountain. Very relaxing.
Worth-It Rating: 2. Add 1 if you're tired.

CAROUSEL OF PROGRESS This was originally designed as part of the 1964 New York World's Fair and has been in continuous operation since then. More people have been on it than any other ride or show anywhere, ever. The technology and concept are a little dated, but the show still holds up. You board a moving theater in the round. As the seats move past each scene, you measure the scientific progress of humanity in this century by the changes in household appliances.
Worth-It Rating: 3

SKYWAY TO FANTASYLAND I never could figure out why this ride was designed to take such a long route to go a short distance. Still, it's your best chance to get aerial photos or video of the parks.

The Fast Track: The line is usually shorter in Tomorrowland.
Worth-It Rating: 3. Add 1 if the line is short.

SPACE MOUNTAIN The world's premier roller coaster is entirely in the dark. It's also one of the best and most enduringly popular rides in the Kingdom.

The Fast Track: The lines are long. Check the line to the left; many times it's shorter. Kids must be 44 inches tall to ride. Don't bother if you get sick easily, are pregnant, or have a weak heart or a bad back.
Worth-It Rating: 5

GRAND PRIX RACEWAY Cars on tracks, no race, no passing, no point. The lines are long, and it's all hot and smelly—I always say that the EPA should close it down because of the air quality. Besides, it's really dated. Go only if the kids won't let you get away. A better bet with the same idea is the Sega race course at Epcot's Innoventions. The simulators there *feel* real, and the race *is* real.

The Fast Track: Kids must be 44 inches tall to drive.
Worth-It Rating: 2

BITES On the days that we arrive in the Magic Kingdom hungry, the place that usually stops us is the **Plaza Pavilion,** a fast foodery that serves pizza and chicken strips. Live shows at nearby Rocket-Tower Plaza make it even more enjoyable. **Auntie Gravity's Galactic Goodies,** near the Grand Prix Raceway, is a pit stop for frozen yogurt and fruit juices. At **Cosmic Ray's Starlight Cafe,** burgers and chicken headline one of the best fast-food menus in the Kingdom. The **Lunching Pad** at

Rocket-Tower Plaza, a little hot-dog stand, is at the base of the AstroOrbiter, right across from Space Mountain.

BUYS **Merchant of Venus** wins my award for the most creatively named store in the park. Just outside Alien Encounter, it specializes in extraterrestrial souvenirs—a lot of little trinkets with holograms, toy rockets, and other space thingies. **Geiger's Counter** is one of a couple of places in the Kingdom where you can get your monogrammed mouse-ears hat.

MICKEY'S TOONTOWN FAIR

This is the only place in the park that gives you continous access to the world's most famous Mouse. Bring your camera and your autograph book and stand in line for a minute with the Mickster. Be ready—cast members try to keep the line moving—and don't ask any tough questions. Mickey, like all Disney characters, is mute. He's allowed to nod (to say yes), shake his head (to say no), and shrug his shoulders ("huh?").

Replacing Mickey's Starland, which opened as Mickey's Birthday Land for Mickey's 60th birthday in 1988, Toontown is all new and incorporates all that the Imagineers have learned over some four decades of creating fun at Disney theme parks. **Worth-It Rating: 3.** Add 2 for children under 10.

MICKEY'S COUNTRY HOUSE AND JUDGE'S TENT Mickey's cartoon world comes alive here. The furniture and Mickey's personal effects are all larger than life. You'll see Mickey's bedroom, his sports equipment, his photos, and his Goofy-remodeled kitchen in your tour of Mickey's very own home on your way to the Toontown County Fair, where you have an appointment with the Toontown Fair's chief judge, Judge Mickey!

MINNIE'S COUNTRY HOUSE The collection of arts and crafts, the charmingly rustic interior, and the manicured garden portray Minnie as Martha Stewart with big ears. Out back, she greets visitors in her garden gazebo.

DONALD'S BOAT In this wet little playground kids can climb and slide on Donald's leaky boat. Little jets of water squirt everywhere, giving kids a chance to cool off on hot days. Personally, I'm neither too old nor too stuffy to stand in the jets myself on a hot day and soak myself well enough to stay cool for several hours. You're at Disney World—be a kid!

TOON PARK Foam animals and a padded floor are undoubtedly lower-maintenance than the live animals of the petting zoo that used to be in this area (I miss Minnie Moo, though, the cow with the Mouse mark on her hide). Kids like climbing on the large, padded animals and bouncing on the thick foam carpet.

TOONTOWN FAIR HALL OF FAME This is a giant gift shop and character encounter where you can send home a box of Florida citrus or stand in line for an autograph and photo with famous characters from classic Disney feature cartoons.

BARNSTORMER AT GOOFY'S WISEACRES FARM The park has needed a ride like this for years—a kid-sized coaster that takes people who can't reach the height bars at the other thrill rides on a barnstorming flight that crashes right through Goofy's giant red barn.

TOONTOWN FAIR TRAIN STATION This is a great place to catch the WDW train. There's seldom a wait.

BUYS The **Duck County Courthouse** sells souvenirs of "Duck Tales" and "Disney Afternoon."

FANTASYLAND

MAD TEA PARTY This giant replica of the Mad Hatter's tea cups from *Alice in Wonderland* is one of my family's favorites. You spin around so fast that you get dizzy. (Okay, so it's a dressed-up carnival standard, too. But it's a great ride with great Disney music and decor.)
Worth-It Rating: 4

MR. TOAD'S WILD RIDE The car that pulls up to take you on this ride might be Mr. Toad's or Badger's or it might have belonged to another character from Disney's adaptation of Kenneth Grahame's *The Wind in the Willows*. The car is just a little kiddie car, and the ride is old and a little dated, with silly stand-up plywood characters, but it's fun! Still one of the best of its kind! And the line moves pretty fast.
Worth-It Rating: 3. Minus 1 if it's crowded.

SNOW WHITE'S ADVENTURES The wicked Queen used to scare the heck out of my kids—and apparently others, too, because she's nearly gone now, the victim of a refurbishing. It's still fairly low-tech, but now you see more of the dwarfs.
Worth-It Rating: 3. Add 1 if you have kids under 10.

CINDERELLA'S GOLDEN CARROUSEL A great big old-fashioned merry-go-round with hand-carved wooden horses that go round and round and up and down to the tunes of famous Disney classics. I think a carousel is a pretty mundane ride for a place like the Magic Kingdom, but my kids have always really loved this ride.

Worth-It Rating: 4. Add 1 if you like carousels.

DUMBO THE FLYING ELEPHANT This is one of the rides that inspired me to create my exclusive Worth-It Ratings. It's really just a short standard carnival ride, and the wait is really long. Stay away unless you have little kids who REALLY love Dumbo *and* the line is short.

Worth-It Rating: 3. Minus 2 if you don't have kids.

LEGEND OF THE LION KING One of the new generation of Disney theater shows, this is just terrific. Life-size puppet figures, great costumes, and dazzling special effects bring the popular movie and its characters to life.

The Fast Track: See my tip about not lining up in Chapter 1.
Worth-It Rating: 5

PETER PAN'S FLIGHT From the time she first spoke, my daughter Tiffany's favorite story was Peter Pan. So we've probably spent enough hours in this line, waiting for our flight in a pirate ship over Neverland, to earn a college degree. Still, Disney's excellent cartoon adaptation of Sir James M. Barrie's timeless tale deserves a better representation than this tired relic of 1950s technology. The lines are too long, the ride is far too short. So sorry.

Worth-It Rating: 2. Add 1 if the line is short, 1 more if your kids are true Peter Pan lovers like Tiffany.

IT'S A SMALL WORLD If you're prone to having silly tunes stuck in your head, beware! (Or wear ear plugs!) You cruise the Small World's waterways as too-cute wooden children on either side of you sing their song over and over—first in English, then in every language spoken since the Tower of Babel. Subtly educational, it's also probably one of the most efficiently designed and best-run attractions anywhere. The lines move nicely, and you wait in air-conditioned comfort. Why can't all the rides work as well?

The Fast Track: Look to the left on the ramp as you go down to the boats. Yes, that's a line—and there's often no one in it!

Worth-It Rating: 5

SKYWAY TO TOMORROWLAND The Skyway goes both ways (*see* Tomorrowland), but I like this Swiss wooden shingled station better than the concrete edifice at the other end (and so, apparently, do a lot of other people, because the line is usually longer here).

Worth-It Rating: 3. Add 1 if the line is short.

BITES Wait! Check out the **Enchanted Grove.** Here's yet another place to get a frozen citrus slushy thing, or an ice cream. **Hook's Tavern** was one of my favorite stops years ago, back when it sold ice-cold grape juice. Now this corner booth next to Peter Pan's Flight features soft drinks. **Lumière's Kitchen,** themed around Jerry Orbach's memorable singing candle in *Beauty and the Beast,* specializes in quick kid's meals. **Pinocchio Village Haus** is one of several spots in the Magic Kingdom that always seem to be downright convenient. Overlooking It's a Small World, it's large and well equipped. The current house specialty is a low-fat turkey dog.

BUYS Fantasyland shops are all clustered together around the Fantasyland entrance to the Cinderella Castle. **Tinker Bell's Treasures** sells children's clothing, including Minnie Mouse dresses and other character outfits. **Mickey's Christmas Carol** is a Christmas store based on Disney's marvelous cartoon adaptation of the Dickens classic (one of our holiday favorites). **Fantasy Faire** specializes in merchandise from recent cartoon classics. The **King's Gallery** is full of medieval-style items. We once bought Tiffany a flowing princess hat here. Like much of our Disney memorabilia, the hat is long gone, but the cherished photo remains. The **Aristocats** sells Disney and other clothing for grown-up children. **Seven Dwarfs' Mining Co.** merchandises items related to the feature film that started it all for Walt in 1937. It's amazing how many cute little character items there are. Many of the treasures featuring Doc, Sleepy, Dopey, Happy, Bashful, Sneezy, and Grumpy and their young surrogate mother have been staples in Disney merchandising for decades.

LIBERTY SQUARE

HAUNTED MANSION This is a spooktacular experience from beginning to end. Don't miss the funny tombstones near the entrance (such as "Here Lies Fred/A Great Big Rock Fell On His Head!"). First you walk, then ride, through a collection of scary scenes that feature every special effect in the Disney's Imagineers' book. Lots of people want to know, in the room that stretches, whether the ceiling is going up, or the floor is going down? The answer is yes! (It's not an elevator, as many believe. The ceiling goes up—just as it seems.)

The Fast Track: Stay to the left, especially in the entrance area. Most people form a line, but actually there's just one big open area and people are expected to fill it up in a mass. Because they don't, you can often go right to the front. Even on crowded days, staffers actually have to ask people to move up. So when you do, just ignore the curmudgeons scowling at you as you pass. When you get to the stretching room, walk straight across to the exit door, so that you can be the first out into the next queue. This is the line for the ride. You'll stand on a moving conveyer belt and step into a moving car. Everyone will be trying to go right; so follow my tip and pass on the left. You could win several valuable Disney minutes—redeemable at the next attraction.

Worth-It Rating: 5

MIKE FINK KEELBOATS Only Elvis and the Beatles approached the popularity of Davy Crockett as he was depicted by Walt Disney on the Disneyland TV show. The episode with Mike Fink and the keelboat race, which this boat ride recalls, was one of the best shows. The Wild West scenery is basically the same thing you see from the riverboats, except that your viewpoint is closer to the water. Don't do both unless you're determined to ride every ride.

Worth-It Rating: 3. Add 1 if there's no line.

LIBERTY SQUARE RIVERBOAT If you've never taken a ride on an old paddle wheeler, this is your chance! It's fun! Especially if you do as I do: Jump on board singing "Old Man River" and ignore all the weird looks from the other passengers. You'll enjoy the great scenery: Despite the fact that you're in Florida, the landscape almost looks like Missouri. And they really do shout "Mark Twain!" At night the river pirates come out, so the boats stop running at dark.

Worth-It Rating: 3. Add 1 if there's no line.

HALL OF PRESIDENTS Abe Lincoln and Bill Clinton both speak during this show, a narration that covers American history as it was made by the nation's presidents. The enormous panoramic film show is followed by a roll call of chief executives. Disney's Audio-Animatronic presidents are very realistic and authentic in every detail, and the show is an asset to any parent trying to instill an interest in history.

Worth-It Rating: 4. Add 1 if you want your children to get a history lesson.

BITES Sleepy Hollow offers vegetarians a nice fast-food menu of salads and sandwiches. And now for my family's four-thumbs-up favorite fast-food stop in the park: **Columbia Harbour House.** Fried fish and chicken baskets are the head-liners, but we go for the rich, hot clam chowder, served in a giant whole-grain bread bowl. Yummy! Also there's **Liberty Tree Tavern**, an old Colonial inn that specializes in hearty fare like pot roast. Dinner is with the characters, lunch is without, and both are by reservation only.

BUYS The **Silversmith** sells gifts and jewelry made of silver or pewter. If you've always wanted a cast pewter Mickey, go no farther. The **Heritage House** offers Americana. My little Ricky, a budding Civil war buff, favors it for its excellent selection of Civil War–era souvenirs. **Olde World Antiques** specializes in Victorian jewelry. And remember *The Legend of Sleepy Hollow*? I do! It was spooky with that headless horse-man, and it's the theme for **Ichabod's**, a magic store that also sells novelties and costume masks.

FRONTIERLAND

Because many of us grew up with Walt Disney, it's easy to forget that he was born at the turn of the last century, the end of the frontier era. The Old West was one of Disney's favorite themes. Its depiction in his Davy Crockett shows was one of his biggest successes.

DIAMOND HORSESHOE REVUE Step right into this saloon and have a root beer! Shows are continuous, dance hall girls sing and dance, and rowdy barkeeps tell jokes. It's a good place to mix food and fun.
Worth-It Rating: 4

FRONTIERLAND SHOOTIN' ARCADE You shoot at moving targets and playful characters in a highly animated gallery with safe, light-powered guns. Ricky loves it.
Worth-It Rating: 2. Add 1 if you have kids.

COUNTRY BEAR JAMBOREE The most fun of all the Audio-Animatronics shows is this Disney version of the Grand Ol' Opry, with 20 full-size singing bears, a moose, and a bison. As many times as we've seen it (dozens), we still howl when Big Al sings "Blood on the Saddle." Lines are reasonable and the waiting air-conditioned, unless the line is out the door.
The Fast Track: Not everybody who's waiting gets into every show, so grab a spot near the doors when you get into the waiting room.
Worth-It Rating: 4. Add 1 if the line is extra short.

TOM SAWYER ISLAND In this re-creation of the world of Tom Sawyer and Huck Finn, a real island in the middle of the Magic Kingdom's lagoon, you can crawl through tunnels, scamper over swaying wooden bridges, and "fahr them guns at Fort Sam Clemens!" (The guns are air-powered, by the way.) There's no light on the island, so regardless of park hours, it closes at dusk.
Worth-It Rating: 3

BIG THUNDER MOUNTAIN RAILROAD The premise here is that a mine train has broken loose from the top of an old mine, and you're on a swooping, plunging, out-of-control ride through the mountains and gorges of Wild West mining country. Steam geysers and water add to the effect.

The Fast Track: Kids must be 40 inches or taller to ride. We usually beat the lines by staying left. There are several water fountains en route; soak your head or your shirt to keep cool.

Worth-It Rating: 4. Add 1 if the line is short.

SPLASH MOUNTAIN This water-coaster, a combination log-flume ride and Audio-Animatronic adventure, is based on *Song of the South,* Disney's take on Joel Chandler Harris's Uncle Remus stories. During your ride with Bre'r Rabbit, Bre'r Bear, and Bre'r Fox, the biggest thrill is the 50-vertical-foot splashdown at the end—which you won't mind a bit on a hot day. The line winds through a maze in the valley beneath the mountain with a few minor sites and sounds like music in the bushes, but Disney could have done a much better job making the line part of the experience. As it is, the lines are long and the wait awful.

The Fast Track: No children under 44 inches tall.

Worth-It Rating: 5

FRONTIERLAND STUNT SHOW Cops and robbers shoot it out in the street in front of the Mile Long Bar (a snack spot). Check your entertainment schedule for times.

Worth-It Rating: 3

BITES Pecos Bill Café is one of the larger fast-food stops, with a spectacular view of Big Thunder Mountain. Out on the street, a stand sells smoked turkey drumsticks. As for the **Mile Long Bar,** it's our favorite place to see the parades.

BUYS Splashdown Photo is the place where you can pick up the photo taken of your family as you plunged down the big drop at the end of the Splash Mountain ride. Even if you don't buy the picture, the instant replay is fun. The **Briar Patch** is also just outside Splash Mountain. It sells gifts based on *Song of the South* as well as Winnie the Pooh merchandise. **Big Al's,** just outside Country Bear Jamboree, sells take-home versions of that show's many popular characters. If you're old enough to remember coonskin caps, you'll be glad that they still have 'em at several shops. **Prairie Outpost & Supply** features native American crafts and *Pocahontas* items. The **Trading Post** specializes in western accessories, while the **Trail Creek Hat Shop** sells hats from one to a full ten gallons. **Frontier Wood Carving** will put your name in oak.

ADVENTURELAND

TROPICAL SERENADE Also known as the Singing Tiki Birds. I dare you to take in this show and leave without its silly melody lodged in your neuro-pathways (as happens to almost everyone at It's A Small World). Dating from 1963, it was the first Audio-Animatronics experience at Disneyland. My family gives it mixed reviews. My wife thinks that the idea of watching mechanical parrots sing and tell bad jokes is for the birds. I love it, as do the kids. Lines are usually short.
Worth-It Rating: 4

PIRATES OF THE CARIBBEAN This also comes from Disneyland. The Florida version is a great place to cool off on a hot day. The lines wind through a fake dungeon that's damp, cool, and full of details that stay with the theme. Then you board a pirate boat that takes you on a wild adventure, through an artillery battle and scenes of a drunken bacchanalia.

The Fast Track: Here, even the wait is great. But time after time we skip the entire line just by keeping left.

Worth-It Rating: 5

JUNGLE CRUISE One of the original Disneyland rides—I remember watching the film of its construction on Walt's TV show back in the mid-50s. The jungle props, plaster pachyderms, and amazing menagerie of other motorized mammals still hold up well after all these years. An open-sided, gas-powered steamer takes you along the Nile and through Southeast Asia, South Africa, and the Amazon rain forest, not necessarily in that order. Watch out for the squirting elephant. Some of the skippers drone, but when they take their comedy seriously, their monologues can be a hoot!

The Fast Track: The winding queue can be the park's worst wait on a hot, muggy day. Before committing yourself to an hour of sweat, park a family member in line while you check out the waiting time. If it's too long, come back when it's cooler. If the park isn't open late, take this ride as early as possible.

Worth-It Rating: 4. Subtract 1 if the line is long.

SWISS FAMILY TREEHOUSE Disney's film *Swiss Family Robinson* has enjoyed a revival thanks to exposure on the Disney Channel and on video to a whole new generation of kids. If you remember the movie, or your kids have seen it on TV, you may want to check out this replica of the house high in a banyan tree that appeared in the motion picture. In my family, we're all afraid of heights, so the steep open climb isn't our cup of tea. Even apart from that, I don't think it's worth the wait, though. You don't do anything and neither does the tree house.

Worth-It Rating: 2

BITES At **Aloha Isle,** the offerings are fruit-juice-based, shake-like things. This is what the tropics are for! In **El Pirata y el Perico,** there's a pirate theme and Mexican fast food like tacos. **Sunshine Tree Terrace** serves more frozen juice concoctions—these made of indigenous citrus.

SHOPPING Most shops cluster in an ersatz bazaar. Stop at **Bwana Bob's** after you find that you just can't live without a stuffed tropical bird. **Elephant Tales** sells safari-themed gifts and clothing, **Traders of Timbuktu** things African. The **Tropics Shop** is your source for Hawaiian shirts and other cliché tropical attire. And check out the **Zanzibar Shell Co.** for sea shells and shell crafts like wind chimes. **House of Treasure** has a pirate theme. I wish I had a nickel for every nickel I spent here during Ricky's pirate period. (And there's more of the same at the **Treasure Chest** and **Lafitte's.**) **Plaza del Sol Caribe Bazaar,** just outside Pirates of the Caribbean, expands your tropical options.

chapter 3

EPCOT CENTER

Walt Disney World

Take I–4 to Exit 26B, Epcot and S.R. 536.

Worth-It Rating: 5
Subtract a point if you have children under 6.

pcot Center is a breathtaking, first-class attraction loved
by millions. Epcot stands for "Experimental Prototype
Community of Tomorrow," an acronym chosen by Walt
Disney to herald a planned community similar to Cele-
bration, the new town Disney is finally building in Kissimmee.
Insiders know that the initials really stand for "Every Person
Comes Out Tired," at this, the biggest of all the theme parks.
I love that joke, because for years, this has been my least
favorite park.

But a funny thing happened while I researched this book.
As I went back again and again, the place won me over.
Maybe my idea of what a theme park should be was too limited. Perhaps I missed the point by simply looking for rides.
Perhaps, being so conscious of value and price, I was overly
annoyed by what I perceived as blatant commercialism. Or
perhaps my vision was clouded by one too many trips with

children who are only now old enough to be excited by the experiences it offers.

Now it's clear to me: Epcot is a place filled with wonder. It may be the only place anywhere that parents can literally take their children around the world and in a single day learn about the cultures of every continent. One can only guess how many future scientists, researchers, and doctors might find the spark that first ignites their passion at Epcot. The bottom line is that Epcot has too many spectacular attractions and cultural experiences to be ignored.

It is also huge. As a result, it seldom feels congested, regardless of the day or season. If you hate crowds, or if the crowds at the other parks get you down, the size may be a plus. And it's ideal on rainy days. Crowds thin out when it rains. And with the right clothes and the right attitude, you have the park mostly to yourself.

TIMING On a weekday in September, when crowds are thin, I went to World Showcase. Mind you, I wasn't even trying to include Future World. Nor did I have kids or family to slow me down. I did not finish before closing time. You won't either. So choose what you want to do, carefully. There's far too much at Epcot for a single day.

EATERTAINMENT AND SHOPPERTOONITIES Particularly in World Showcase, food and shopping are an integral part of the experience. To take advantage of many of Epcot's best features, you have to spend more money than in any other park.

THE LAY OF THE LAND Epcot is like a barbell. You enter on the bottom, in Future World. World Showcase is at the top of the barbell, with pavilions along the World Showcase Promenade, which rings a central lagoon. World Showcase's American Adventure, in the middle of the top loop, is directly opposite Spaceship Earth, and Epcot's signature geosphere, at the bottom of Future World, is straight ahead of you when you go through the entrance turnstiles.

THE FAST TRACK Because Future World opens first, I suggest you begin there. Lines will be long. So do the things that don't have lines, such as Innoventions. Head to World Showcase a little before it opens, even if you're not finished in Future World. Begin in Mexico and work clockwise to Canada. Remember, the earlier you get to World Showcase, the thinner the crowds. (Conversely, crowds thin out in Future World later in the day.)

Future World

SPACESHIP EARTH

SPACESHIP EARTH RIDE A discovery-type ride, where the thrills are all for the mind, this is a brief history of the world from dinosaurs to spaceships. Always a favorite of ours, it's even better now, with 15 new scenes.
The Fast Track: You'll often find short lines, particularly late in the day. If you arrive early and it's crowded, skip it and come back before you leave.
Worth-It Rating: 5

INNOVENTIONS EAST AND WEST

What's new in the world? This is where you can see the latest in gimmicks and gadgets and try out nifty new things like virtual reality.

Stop in for a multi-media trip through the history of innovation and invention with Bill Nye the Science Guy. Then try out a new wrist telephone from AT&T. Check out the latest software, and play with animation on a Silicon Graphics workstation. Have your camcorder handy: At the GE exhibit there's a nifty spot where you can be interviewed by Jay Leno through the magic of electronic special effects. My son, Ricky, would be completely happy to spend the entire day at Sega's exhibit. Its full-size road race is everything the Magic Kingdom's Grand Prix raceway always wanted to be—a wild, jolting simulator where you can pass, skid, spin out, and actually compete to win against other drivers. Too bad it costs an extra four bucks.

Also check out the leaping fountain and live entertainment from **Future Corps.** Everything is high-tech, including the streetmosphere by **Kristos Acrobats,** talking **EpBOTS** robots, and the impromptu cacaphonous comedic concerts by **Jammitors.** Mickey, Minnie, and other Disney characters make frequent appearances in metallic, space-age attire. Signs throughout the park show the time and place for character appearances.

Worth-It Rating: 5

BITES Go for sandwiches and chicken at the **Electric Umbrella,** pasta and pizza at the **Pasta Piazza. Fountain View** serves espresso and baked goods.

THE LIVING SEAS

The giant aquarium in the middle of the pavilion is not keeping the folks at Sea World up at night, but you'll see a fairly impressive collection of undersea life, including sharks and manatees, plus exhibits on aquatic exploration and a ride "through the ocean depths."
Worth-It Rating: 3

BITES You'll feel like you're inside the aquarium as you gaze through the 8-foot glass windows at the **Coral Reef Restaurant,** a seafood restaurant that's one of the most popular Disney dining spots (reservations essential). And if you've ever wanted to see Mickey Mouse underwater, this is the place; see him at the restaurant's character breakfast.

THE LAND

LISTEN TO THE LAND This little boat ride about agri-science is fun and informative for school-age children.
Worth-It Rating: 4

GREENHOUSE TOUR They use hydroponics and other high-tech tricks to grow their own veggies in The Land greenhouses, and on this 45-minute guided walk, you see how. Whether or not this is worth the trouble depends entirely in your interest in the science of agriculture. Reserve at the pavilion.

HARVEST THEATER The "Circle of Life" film that plays here is a harmless little presentation on taking care of Mother Earth, featuring the *The Lion King* gang.
Worth-It Rating: 3

FOOD ROCKS This show is like It's a Small World with singing veggies. Little kids love it.
Worth-It Rating: 4

BITES The **Garden Grill,** a revolving full-service restaurant, overlooks some of the scenery you see in the Listen to the Land boat ride. Reserve ahead. The **Sunshine Season Food Fair,** an elaborate food court, gives you home-style cooking with natural and organic ingredients. Try the vegetable lasagna at the **Cheese Store.**

JOURNEY INTO IMAGINATION

This pavilion explores the creative process.

MAGIC EYE THEATER *Honey, I Shrunk the Audience!,* which plays here, is the best show at Epcot and my pick for second-best 3D show in the world (after *Terminator 2 3D* at Universal). A 3D sequel to the films, *Honey I Shrunk and/or Blew Up the Kids and/or the Baby,* it gets actor Rick Moranis to shrink the entire audience. You're subsequently menaced by giant reptiles. Don't miss it!
Worth-It Rating: 5

IMAGE WORKS A pretty nifty creative playground featuring hands-on experiences with "creative playthings" that demonstrate technology ranging from computer graphics to static electricity.
Worth-It Rating: 4

JOURNEY INTO IMAGINATION RIDE Spend a mildly amusing 13 minutes with Figment, the purple dragon who's Epcot's quasi-mascot, and his pal, Dreamfinder.
Worth-It Rating: 3

GM WORLD OF MOTION

In this GM booster, a blockbuster roller coaster slated to become Epcot's best ride is scheduled to replace the merry little ride that used to occupy the space.

TEST TRACK Only Disney creates the kind of combination thrill ride and visual experience that you find at Splash Mountain and the other adventure-coasters. This new one, not yet open as I write, promises to be the best, longest, and fastest ever. The high drama derives from bad weather, hazardous road conditions, and high speed.

WONDERS OF LIFE

One of our favorite stops at Epcot, this has a large center court full of activities that remind me of Innoventions. But here the themes are life, health, and fitness.

BODY WARS A simulator ride, similar to Star Tours at Disney–MGM Studios, except that you're on a synthetic trip into a human being. Your simulator is shrunk and injected into a person (much like Martin Short is in *Inner Space*). The family and I agree that this one is a little too rough.

The Fast Track: Children under 48 inches, people with heart and back problems, and women who are pregnant are advised not to ride. Unfortunately, there's no fast track, and the lines are usually long.

Worth-It Rating: 4

CRANIUM COMMAND An absolutely charming and wonderfully funny Audio-Animatronic show-cum-movie that takes you inside the brain of a 12-year-old boy. The star-studded comic cast includes many TV favorites as operators of vital organs.

The Fast Track: The entrance is hidden at the back of Wonders of Life, so many people miss the show and lines are often short. Before you get in, you'll be routed into a holding area with a movie. There, look for the doors to the show's theater and get as close to them as you can. All seats are good, but the front is the best.

Worth-It Rating: 5

THE MAKING OF ME After you've seen this movie about how babies develop, you may want to start that little "birds and bees" talk with your kids. Or maybe not. In any case, be prepared. This Martin Short film is fairly explicit, and the fetus footage is graphic.

Worth-It Rating: 3. Add 2 if you want Martin Short to explain the facts of life to your children.

CENTER COURT All kinds of great activities are here. At the **Coach's Corner,** you can evaluate your golf, tennis, or baseball skills. **Wondercycles** give you a quick little workout, along with an instant analysis of the calories burned in various thrilling simulated situations. In cartoon/live action **Goofy about Health** show, the great Goofy demonstrates why you should get your potato off the couch. The **Anacomical Players** improvise skits about health. The **Lifestyle Revue** gives you the chance to rate the healthiness of your lifestyle (or in my case, the lack thereof). Finally, the **Sensory Funhouse** lets you test your six senses (the sixth being your sense of humor). One of the activities is sticking your hand into a hole in a box, then trying to figure out what you're touching. Most people guess wrong.

BITES **Pure and Simple** has health-smart fast food such as waffles, yogurt, sandwiches, and salads.

UNIVERSE OF ENERGY

We love this attraction, every time we come! It now features Ellen DeGeneres, Jamie Lee Curtis, and Bill Nye the Science Guy, with a cameo appearance by the late Dr. Albert Einstein, in a simulated game of Jeopardy. The entire auditorium moves on a track through a primeval forest filled with life-size Audio-Animatronic dinosaurs. It's a multi-media extravaganza that's funny, informative, and absolutely spectacular.
Worth-It Rating: 5

World Showcase

This is Disney's ongoing, permanent world's fair where, in a single day, you can capture Kodak moments in front of most of the world's major landmarks.

Not every country in the world is included. Don't look for politics, either: all political content has been removed for your protection.

SHOPPERTOONITIES AND EATERTAINMENT Even if you don't buy anything, take the time to browse in the shops. Nowhere else in the world will you find such a diverse international offerings in a single place. And each country's pavilion featuring its native cuisine in fast fooderies and great sit-down restaurants. As in all parks, the food is pricey. But the presentations are world-class, so the overall experience is memorable. Reservations are almost always required (tel. 407/824–4321 for information, Disney Dining at 407/939–3463 to reserve).

STREETMOSPHERE "Streetmosphere" is what Disney calls those roaming costumed character actors who help create the mood. **World-Class Brass** performs pop music with a little comedy throughout World Showcase. Ditto for the **Junkanoo Bus,** a wildly painted Caribbean contraption that not only plays music but has an on-board bar that serves tropical drinks (in Future World, too)!

THE UNITED KINGDOM

You'll see what's so great about Britain in this miniature replication featuring formal English gardens, a traditional English herb garden and maze, and a cobblestone street lined with Tudor homes and Victorian buildings. Phone home: the old-fashioned red telephone booths really work. The garden by the lake can be a great place to see IllumiNations.

Bites: At the **Rose & Crown,** you'll find traditional British fare. Here's your big chance to try kidney pie (or stick with fish and chips and British brews). Reserve ahead.

Buys: The **Toy Soldier** sells British toys. **Lords and Ladies** is all perfume and tobacco, the **Tea Caddy** all teas and teapots. **Pringle of Scotland** stocks Scottish woolens. Ever since Ricky saw *Braveheart,* he's been fascinated with Scottish culture. Each clan has its own plaid, and the selection here represents most of them. You'll also find real bagpipes, practice pipes, how-to tapes, and piper music. The **Magic of Wales** and **The Queen's Table** sell decorative items.

Streetmosphere: Check out the **World Showcase Players.** Guests help with the skits. And look for the roving bagpipers. When I told them that Ricky wanted to learn to play, we were treated to a concert with instruction—wonderful!

Worth-It Rating: 4

NORWAY

The ornate architecture of a 14th-century Norwegian fortress and a 12th-century stave church make this one of the most visually entertaining spots in World Showcase. The church houses Norwegian art and artifacts.

Maelstrom: My daughter Tiffany's favorite ride in World Showcase is a stormy trip in a Viking ship with great Audio-Animatronic bears and more. But the ending is abrupt; one minute you're in the middle of a stormy northern sea, the next you're climbing out of your boat.

Bites: Norwegians invented the smorgasbord, so it should come as no surprise that they do it so well at **Restaurant Akershus,** with good hot and cold entrées and all the herring you'd expect. You'll feel like a Viking at the rough wooden tables among the stone walls of what could be an ancient Norse castle. Reserve ahead.

Buys: The **Puffin's Roost,** just outside Maelstrom, sells clothing, toys, and candy, including one of the world's most extensive selections of trolls.

Worth-It Rating: 5

CANADA

Indian totem poles in a scene straight out of the old Northwest Mountie movies welcome you to the Great White North! Framed by a Disney version of Canadian mountains are a waterfall and replica of Ottawa's imposing Château Laurier. In the foreground, Disney has re-created British Columbia's spectacularly floral Butchart Gardens.

O Canada!: This movie contains a lot of purple mountains' majesty. I love these CircleVision 360 movies. You're completely surrounded by curved screens, which literally put you in the center of the action. But there are no seats, and nothing but a guard rail to lean on. I'd like the thrilling toboggan ride, powerful audio, and spectacular views a whole lot more if I didn't have to stand.

Bites: With its big, low stone arches, **Le Cellier** looks like a fancy cellar restaurant, but the hearty prime rib, turkey, and shepherd's pie are served cafeteria style, along with salads and desserts. It's my kind of place—and not a bad deal.

Buys: **Northwest Mercantile** is like a log cabin, stocked with Native American crafts. **Le Boutique** sells French-Canadian jewelry, fragrances, and novelties.

Streetmosphere: Canada is another place where Ricky can find bagpipes—look for both the **Caledonia Bagpipes** and the **Pipes of Nova Scotia.** You may also run into the **Cana-**

dian Comedy Corps, who remind you how funny Canadians can be.
Worth-It Rating: 3

FRANCE

Here you enter a rural French neighborhood from the 1600s. The Eiffel Tower is the park's best photo op.

Impressions of France: During this 18-minute wide-screen tour of France, you ride, slide, and fly through Paris and the French countryside to the strains of music by classical French composers, played over an excellent sound system.

Bites: Wouldn't you expect great French food here? At **Les Chefs de France,** three world-class chefs run the restaurant (Paul Bocuse, Roger Vergé, and Gaston Lenôtre). Some of the dishes are awesome. **Bistro de Paris** is our favorite Epcot restaurant. Terrie, my wife, loves the French onion soup, and we both endorse the rack of lamb for two. At **Au Petit Café,** you can just pop in and grab a quiche, a croissant, or a chunk of French bread and cheese. If you arrive late in the evening, the meal comes with a reasonable view of IllumiNations from a comfortable seat. Reserve for all.

Buys: Pâté anyone? Check **Le Mode Français.** For fragrances, it's **La Signature,** for cosmetics the **Guerlain Boutique,** for wine **La Maison du Vin. Plume et Palette** has art and crystal (watch the kids). With youngsters, you're better off in **Galerie des Halles** (or maybe not—it sells toys and candy). Look for the *Hunchback of Notre Dame* booth. Where else would it be?

Streetmosphere: **Gordoon,** a clown with a Maurice Chevalier accent, improvises with children and seltzer. It's wet, wild, and wonderful. And although gypsies aren't French, France does have gypsies. The **Tzigantzi** troupe performs their songs and dances, while Left Bank portrait artists paint you while you wait nearby.

Worth-It Rating: 4

MOROCCO

This is a finely detailed reproduction of the cities of North Africa, only a lot cleaner. Fez House and the Nejjarine Fountain are both replicas of famous structures, and there's an interesting exhibit of Moroccan art. But where's Rick's American Café?

Bites: North Africans consider lamb to be the best of all meats. At **Restaurant Marrakesh,** beef, chicken, and fish also go with the couscous, but it's never as good with the substitutions. While you dine, the Casablanca Fez Belly Dancers and Musicians gyrate. You'll need reservations.

Buys: Carpets, clothing, and crafts spill out the doors and into the street in true bazaar style. **Marketplace in the Medina, Casablanca Carpets, Tangier Traders, the Brass Bazaar, Medina Arts,** and the **Berber Oasis** are a great place to pick up hand-crafted Moroccan brass and leather goods. At the edge of the pavilion, clever Disney marketers have set up an Aladdin shop.

Streetmosphere: Keep your ears open for the bellydancers and folk musicians. Wow. The **Houzali Troupe** performs in the courtyard by the lagoon—four drums, a flute, and one very nice belly.

Worth-It Rating: 3. Add 1 if you plan to shop here.

JAPAN

The real Japan is tiny and overcrowded, the land highly prized, and the gardens precious. So the centerpiece of Epcot's Japan is a spectacular re-creation of a classic Japanese garden. You'll also see a replica five-story pagoda dating from the eighth century, Nara's Temple of Horyuji. An art exhibit is housed in a reproduction of a medieval stone castle surrounded by a moat.

Bites: In the **Teppanyaki Rooms,** you sit at tables that wrap around big grills where chefs chop up meat and veggies before your eyes. If you've been to Benihana, you know the drill. **Tempura Kiku** specializes in batter-fried fare. Reserve ahead for both. **Yakitori House** serves Nipponese fast food. The teriyaki beef and chicken dishes, the yummy red bean dessert, and the children's menu rate a mention.

Buys: One of Japan's leading merchants, **Mitsukoshi,** offers the best of the wares from its department stores—great kimonos and Japanese dolls as well as lacquer ware, oriental fabrics, karate suits, samarai swords, jewelry, carvings, paintings, and a zillion knick-knacks.

Streetmosphere: **One World Taiko** consists of two drummers beating out those great old ancient Japanese tunes. **Matsur-izi,** which is larger, also performs Japanese percussive music. The bizarre troupe known as **Cirikili** are "stilt birds"—Japanese actor/acrobats on high stilts who wear mechanical bird contraptions that make them look like warriors astride giant metallic ostriches. Think Shogun meets Star Wars.

Worth-It Rating: 3. Add 1 if you plan to eat here.

THE AMERICAN ADVENTURE

The focal point of this pavilion is a magnificent colonial structure that's a little like Philadelphia's Independence Hall and Williamsburg's Governor's Mansion in one, with touches of the White House and the Capitol.

American Adventure Show: This really is the best show in the World Showcase, and I'm not just being patriotic. Audio-Animatronic Ben Franklin and Mark Twain host this dazzling half hour. It's Disney's best Audio-Animatronic show, period. The figures are so lifelike that at times they look and sound real. The montage of scenes from America's past may moisten your eyes, as they do mine.

Bites: No funny stuff at the **Liberty Inn.** Just strictly American burgers, hot dogs, and fries.

Buys: Hit **Heritage Manor** for cutesy American country-style gifts. The selection of American flag novelties (I collect 'em) is one of the best I've seen anywhere, even Washington, D.C., and Philadelphia.

Streetmosphere: The **Voices of Liberty** sing a capella in the waiting area for the show. Or try to catch the **Sons of Liberty,** a traditional fife and drum corps. The **American Gardens Theater,** across the promenade from the pavilion, features concerts and celebrity appearances; check the schedule near the stage.

Worth-It Rating: 5

MEXICO

A carving of the serpent-god Quetzalcoatl presides over the steps of this imposing reproduction Maya temple. Inside, there's an impressive display of pre-Columbian primitive art. And in the plaza in the center of the pavilion is crammed with Mexican novelties. In perpetual twilight, the plaza is always cool and dark—an excellent refuge from hot, muggy afternoons. The front steps are one of the better places to see IllumiNations.

El Rio del Tiempo: The pavilion's main feature is this ride (the name translates as "river of time"), which takes you through representations of the history of Mexico from ancient cultures to the present. Don't look for anything spectacular, and if the wait looks long, move on.

Bites: The setting of the **San Angel Inn Restaurant,** overlooking the River of Time ride, is one of the most romantic in the park. Lavish margueritas contribute to the mood. On the menu, along with predictable enchiladas and tacos, are unexpected selections like mahi-mahi and grilled shrimp. Reserve ahead. I call the **Cantina de San Angel** "Taco Tinker Bell" (get it?). Its waterfront veranda is a good viewpoint for IllumiNations, and the kids like the churros—crispy, cinnamon Mexican sweets. I recommend the generously sized margueritas. Ricky says that the watermelon juice, which you can buy by the cup, is the best he's ever had.

Buys: Deep in the interior of the pavilion is the **Plaza de los Amigos,** where you can walk among carts filled with castanets, hand-made Mexican dolls, pottery, jewelry, ponchos, straw hats, leather goods, even tequila. **Artesanias Mexicanas,** Mexican glass blowers, make tiny animals and characters in glass on up to big, ornate, overpriced, overblown doojamahickees that are definitely not for kids; you can also buy pottery, candles, and other less easily destructible crafts.

Streetmosphere: **Mariachi Cobre,** a 10-piece horns-and-string ensemble, serenades guests on the veranda and in the pavilion with the kind of traditional Mexican music most of us best remember from the old gunslinger movies. **Huitzilin,** a native American drum and wind group, involves guests in stories, dances, and songs.

Worth-It Rating: 4

ITALY

An ornate fountain and a tall brick tower dominate the classic plaza, a reproduction of St. Mark's Square.

Bites: If you've never had fettucine Alfredo perfectly prepared, you should try it at the elegant **L'Originale Alfredo di Roma Ristorante**, a re-creation of the restaurant that originated it (reservations a must). Strolling musicians serenade under the spectacular chandeliers, and the fresh pasta is made right before your very mouth. Not a pizza in sight!

Buys: **Il Bel Cristallo** sells Venetian glass, jewelry, leather, and Capodimonte ceramics—those large, shiny ceramic objects covered with pink flowers and painted angels made famous by the Home Shopping Network. **La Cucina** stocks Italian edibles, wines, and cooking implements. **Delizie Italiane** sells Italian sweets. Pinocchio anyone? His shop is here, too.

Streetmosphere: You might encounter **I Cantanapoli**, a street quartet from Naples, playing all your Neapolitan favorites.

Worth-It Rating: 4

GERMANY

A statue of St. George slays a statue of a dragon in the square, surrounded by the gingerbread rooftops.

Bites: The raucous **Biergarten** has an all-you-can-eat buffet—look for me! The wurst is the best! Roast chicken, dumplings, kraut, and potato salad round out the spread. Imported beers in quart steins that look like pitchers are served to revelers sitting at long, wooden tables. And there's non-stop live oompah music, plus yodeling, a glockenspiel, giant alpine horns, and a serenading saw. **Sommerfest** serves German fast food. Try a brat with kraut, mein frau!

Buys: Look for German sweets, beer steins, cuckoo clocks, hand-carved wooden nutcrackers, and other Christmas items. A nutcracker nut, Ricky certifies the selection as the best he's seen (I certify that it's certainly not the cheapest). Check out **Der Bücherwurm** and its beautiful hand-painted eggs; the stuffed stuff and dolls at **Der Teddybär**; and the fine German crystal at **Kunstarbeit in Kristall.**

Streetmosphere: The **Alpine Trio,** consisting of a guitarist, a tuba player, and an accordionist, make frequent appearances. **Worth-It Rating: 3.** Add 1 if you want to eat a lot.

AFRICA

This exhibit includes a shop called the **Village Trader** and some African entertainment performed in tribal costumes. What is here is good. But there's not enough to represent the heritage of African-Americans.
Worth-It Rating: 5

CHINA

A garden-ringed Temple of Heaven dominates this pavilion. There's also a fine display of ancient imperial art, largely from the collection of Beijing's Palace Museum and San Francisco's Avery Brundage Collection.

Wonders of China: This CircleVision 360 movie skips the sweat shops. But it's Chinese torture to endure this 20-minute show with no seating—everyone stands, and only lean rails are provided. But if you don't mind, you may enjoy this fairly impressive production; it will give you a wide view of the breathtaking geography and varied cultures of this enormous country.

Bites: The beautifully appointed **Nine Dragons** features regional cuisine from all major Chinese provinces. **Lotus Blossom Café** is the place to pick up a quick egg roll, sweet-and-sour chicken, stir-fried beef, or wonton soup. Prices are reasonable, and the food is very good.

Buys: **Yong Feng Shangdian** is China's own Macy's. Much of what you see is predictable—lots of silk and knick-knacks. Other offerings are surprising, including several pieces only Michael Eisner could afford.

Streetmosphere: In the courtyard, the **Pu Yang Acrobats** and the **Flying Dragon Variety Troupe** perform amazing feats of balance and agility. **China Si Zhu** is the warmup for *Wonders of China*: A performer tells stories of Chinese history while playing the flute, zither, or dulcimer.

Worth-It Rating: 4

ILLUMINATIONS

Mark Fisher, designer for Rolling Stones and Pink Floyd shows, has made this night show faster and hipper, with more lights, music, and fireworks than ever before. Unfortunately, the presentation still can't overcome the venue's limitations. No matter where I am, I always feel I'm missing most of the show. When you can see it, what you see is laser lights dancing on Spaceship Earth, turning it into a giant globe and lasers lighting up the lagoon with a rousing sound track. I can't even imagine how great it would be if I *could* see everything.

chapter 4

DISNEY–MGM STUDIOS THEME PARK

Walt Disney World

Take I–4 to Exit 26B, S.R. 536 and Epcot.

Worth-It Rating: 5-
It's very nice, but not quite Universal.

Disney has done an excellent job of reinventing the movie park, a genre invented by Universal Studios. While both parks try to capture the spirit of the studios of Hollywood's Golden Age, Disney–MGM is not so much a replica of an old-time Hollywood studio as a caricature of one—specifically, the one Disney created so successfully for the film *Who Framed Roger Rabbit*.

The park is wonderfully detailed. As you enter, you'll pass a filling station parked up with vintage cars and replete with oil cans, gas pumps, and spare parts dating from the 40s. The collectibles store across the street, **Sid Cahuenga's One-of-a-Kind,** is like a museum full of Hollywood memorabilia. Many of these items cost more than your entire vacation. And others you can take home for a song (well, almost).

What does Disney have to do with MGM? Almost nothing: there's never been a Disney–MGM film. But at the time that corporate raider Kirk Kerkorian was disassembling the old MGM, Disney was in need of material for its movie park. And the rest is history.

Comparisons are inevitable when you write about two movie parks in the same book. Many of the rides and shows at Disney–MGM are similar to those at Universal Studios Florida, but toned down—Universal-Lite. Catastrophe Canyon on the Backstage Studio Tour at Disney–MGM, and Universal's Earthquake: The Big One, are almost identical. But the explosion and flood at Catastrophe Canyon are not nearly as terrifying as those at Universal. Disney–MGM's Star Tours and Universal's Back to the Future are both action-simulator rides. But the Back to the Future screen, 90 feet tall, is bigger than the one at a drive-in theater; the Star Tours screen seems smaller than that at your local mall's multiplex.

The strengths of the Disney park are its cartoon and children's attractions. Those themed around the late Jim Henson's incredibly popular Muppets and the movie *Honey, I Shrunk the Kids* make the park a must-see for families. Disney's incredible string of animated hits are all brought to life with wonderful stage shows, seen only at this park. These shows are the best in any theme park, Broadway class. Another highlight is the "streetmosphere," strolling character actors pretending to be starlets, agents, and other vintage Hollywood types; interacting with guests, they add immeasurably to the sense of place.

TIMING You won't be able to do all you want to do in a day, but it's going to be fun to try!

EATERTAINMENT Restaurant meals and fast food here make for terrific themed experiences. You can't count on getting in unless you've booked well in advance (tel. 407/939–3463 or 407/WDW–DINE).

SHOPPERTOONITIES If you remember my rule to shop in the parks only for what's unavailable elsewhere, you'll look for movie memorabilia, from autographs to animation cells, at prices that range from "Wow, what a deal!" to "If you really want it, honey, I guess we could sell the house."

TV SHOW TAPINGS The **Production Information Window,** at the main entrance, dispenses tickets for shows that require an audience. But it's better to call ahead to find out what will be taping when and then schedule accordingly. Also ask how long the taping will take: to make even a half-hour show can easily take half a day or more—and really cut into your theme-park time. Depending on the show, you will have to grab a seat or a place in line early, and wait; bring snacks to help pass the time and beat the heat.

THE FAST TRACK My advice is to do all the attractions that involve walking first. The Magic of Animation, the Back Lot Tour, and the Honey, I Shrunk the Kids adventure playground are much more enjoyable without sore feet. Plus, most people run for the rides first thing, so they're less crowded later in the day.

THE LAY OF THE LAND As you enter, you walk straight down Hollywood Boulevard. Sunset Boulevard is off to your right, Echo Lake to your left. Ahead of you, roughly on the left, is New York Street; Mickey Avenue is ahead and slightly to the right.

HOLLYWOOD BOULEVARD AND ECHO LAKE

A replica of Grauman's Chinese Theater, the scene of most of the major Hollywood premieres in the good old days, is straight ahead, dominating the park's skyline. On your left as you face it is a small lake, around which the park has re-created LA's Echo Park, a picturesque oasis used as a location for several B movies.

GREAT MOVIE RIDE The lobby of this Disney version of Hollywood's most famous landmark is full of memorabilia—most notably Dorothy's original ruby-red slippers. Beyond is a fast-moving adventure full of wild surprises. Actually, a tram takes you through scenes from the *Wizard of Oz, Mary Poppins,* and many other great films, featuring Audio-Animatronic replicas of screen idols such as John Wayne, Jimmy Cagney, and Edward G. Robinson. I won't spoil it for you except to say that it really *is* a great movie ride.
The Fast Track: Lines vary more than any I've seen. Sometimes there's none, and sometimes the line is very, very long. If it looks like you'll have to wait, come back later.
Worth-It Rating: 5

INDIANA JONES STUNT SPECTACULAR I was picked! Many volunteer, but few are chosen, and I was actually chosen to play a bad guy in the exploding airplane scene in *Raiders of the Lost Ark.* This tightly choreographed demonstration of stunt magic and acrobatics includes the race with the giant boulder from the same movie. The wait is long and boring. Be patient.
Worth-It Rating: 5

SUPERSTAR TELEVISION & MONSTER SOUND SHOW Combined, these two attractions are very similar to *Murder, She*

Wrote at Universal. But here, instead of a single experience, there are two lines and two waits. At both, arrive early, since before each show a producer chooses some of the most enthusiastic spectators to be in the production. Superstar Television demonstrates visual effects with clips from TV series such as *I Love Lucy, Cheers, Home Improvement,* the *Tonight Show with Johnny Carson,* and the *Late Show with David Letterman;* the real action is on TV monitors overhead. Monster Sound Show, which explains how the audio portion of our program gets there, features Chevy Chase and Martin Short in a silly little film that gets even sillier when the audience provides the audio.

Worth-It Rating: 3

STAR TOURS Okay, I keep saying it's a lot smaller than Universal's Back to the Future. But it's still a great ride. And it's not as rough. As the story goes, your shuttle to the moon of Endor is piloted by a rookie robot of monumental ineptitude—and that's where the thrills begin. The waiting area is part of the experience, with exceptional entertainment value—and air-conditioning.

The Fast Track: Be on the lookout for a second line. When you first enter, you'll be in a robot and spacecraft repair area with a steep ramp. Apparently, it's not obvious to everyone that there are usually two lines.

Worth-It Rating: 5

BITES Every showbiz eatery worth its salt has caricatures on the walls, and why should the **Brown Derby** be an exception? The setting is stylish and faintly deco, and the menu is straightforward American steaks, seafood, and pastas. Get a reservation in advance or go early. At **Starring Rolls,** near the Brown Derby, Nestle and the famous Toll House cookie invite you to ignore your diet. The **Prime Time Cafe** makes you wonder: Is it dinner time or showtime? A woman claiming to be your mother brings you meatloaf and insists that you eat your veggies, as tableside TVs play clips in beautiful black and white. Come with reservations. **Hollywood & Vine Cafeteria,** next door, is your typical 50s cafeteria—convenient and reasonably priced. My son, Ricky, loves the ribs. It's a big place, so lines are usually manageable. At this **Commissary,** behind Superstar Television, look for burgers, fries, and chicken sandwiches.

On the shore of Echo Lake, you'll find **Dinosaur Gertie's Ice Creams of Extinction,** cleverly shaped like a dinosaur whose nose appears to smoke—courtesy of the cold air in the freezer. **Min & Bill's Dockside Diner** is another giant prop you just can't miss, an old gray ship where you'll find snacks like yogurt, frozen fruit, and juices.

Backlot Express, between Star Tours and Indiana Jones, is another fast foodery. Or how about dinner in a '57 Chevy convertible served by a car-hop at the drive-in theater? Try the **Sci-Fi Dine-In Theater.** Terrie, my wife, always goes for burgers, fries, and a shake.

BUYS Disney never misses a chance to put themed merchandise in your face. **Movieland Merchandise** and **Crossroads of the World,** near the entrance, sell movie-theme souvenirs—and lots of candy in film cans.

Look to the left as you enter the park, and you'll see **Sid Cahuenga's One-of-a-Kind.** You might even see Sid, dressed in his safari outfit, rocking on the porch of his shop. Just to your right as you enter the park is **Oscar's Classic Car Souvenirs & Super Service,** the reproduction gas station. It's stocked with the kind of toy cars and trinkets you might have found at the original. **Darkroom,** nearby, handles photo stuff.

Heading down the Boulevard, you'll pass **Mickey's of Hollywood, Pluto's Toy Palace, Disney & Co,** and **LA Cin-**

ema Storage, which sell Disney and Disney–MGM logo merchandise—and it ain't just T-shirts and mouse ears anymore. At **Cover Story,** you'll get your picture on the cover of a fictitious magazine. **Celebrity 5 & 10,** a takeoff on a vintage Woolworth store, fascinated my children as an example of how it was way back when Dad was a kid. **Keystone Clothiers** is stuffed with Beverly Hills–style outfits (with prices to match), all to give you that vintage Tinseltown look. **Lakeside News,** near the lake, showcases magazines with the emphasis on new and old showbiz titles.

Returning from Endor, you pass through **Endor Vendors,** loaded with Star Wars souvenirs and space toys. We found Ricky's light saber with sound effects here, and my own Darth Vader mask. Ricky loves the **Indiana Jones Adventure Outpost** stand, which offers rubber snakes, many variations on Indie's trademark hat, and more.

NEW YORK STREET

A technique known as "forced perspective" allows film makers to fake big-city skylines without leaving the lot. New York Street, the perfect example of how it works, was used in *Dick Tracy* and other films.

JIM HENSON'S MUPPET VISION 4D This is a great show! Spectacularly silly, it's complete with exploding walls, rain from the ceiling, pies in the face, and lots of other slapstick featuring all the Muppets you know and love along with a weird flying character created especially for this show.
The Fast Track: If you sit too close to the front, you'll miss some of the best laughs (look for old guys in the box seats!).
Worth-It Rating: 5

HONEY, I SHRUNK THE KIDS MOVIE SET ADVENTURE This free-form playground is a great place to cool off. You climb and slide on giant grass and trash, just like in the movie but with water squirting everywhere.
Worth-It Rating: 4. Add 1 if the line is short, as it often is.

BITES **Mama Melrose's Ristorante Italiano** fits the New York theme perfectly, with pizzas baked in a brick oven, pasta, steak, and seafood. You need reservations.

MICKEY AVENUE AND
THE ANIMATION COURTYARD

Here are the Disney studio's working sound stages, where you may find shows and/or films in progress.

INSIDE THE MAGIC: SPECIAL EFFECTS AND PRODUCTION TOUR You walk through a working sound stage and see the action through big glass windows (*not* one-way glass). If you wave, an actor might wave back—I did and he did.
Worth-It Rating: 4

VOYAGE OF THE LITTLE MERMAID Ariel and Sebastian lead an all-starfish cast in this live adaptation of the Disney cartoon feature. Glowing, floaty, black-lit characters, a cool mist emanating from the ceiling, and a gee-whiz bubble machine make you feel truly sub-marine. Remember back in 1992 when a 21-year-old college student named Leanza Cornett, playing the heroine here at the time, went from Ariel's throne to win the Miss America pageant? The stars are still that good.
Worth-It Rating: 5

WALT DISNEY THEATER In this cool movie theater, you can sit down for half an hour and see made-for-The-Disney-Channel movies about Disney films.
Worth-It Rating: 3

BACKSTAGE STUDIO TOUR Ironically, this is more like the original Universal Studios Hollywood tour than anything at Universal Studios Florida. It's part self-guided walking tour, part tram ride through production, wardrobe, props areas, a soundstage, and an exhibit area or two; you cruise a residential street where you'll easily recognize the homes of Beaver, the Golden Girls, the Empty Nest gang, and more—but there are no buildings behind the facades. The Catastrophe Canyon section of the tour features an exploding gas truck and a flood similar to the one at Universal's Earthquake: The Big One (but not nearly as scary). However, it's a more impressive production with an in-depth explanation of the earthquake/explosion/flood effect that Earthquake lacks.
The Fast Track: Lines are long. Do it early or late in the day. The wait may be shorter, and the heat of the blast from the fire is really miserable in afternoon heat.
Worth-It Rating: 5

MAGIC OF DISNEY ANIMATION You see the artists working on future Disney animated films on this self-guided multimedia tour of the art on which the empire was built. On display are drawings and cells from Disney classics.
Worth-It Rating: 5

BITES The **Soundstage** food court—decorated with props, giant movie lights, rigging, and other film artifacts—is the park's largest eatery. Character breakfasts are available by reservation in the morning. Above, you can sip alcoholic beverages high in the rigging at the **Catwalk Bar**. At **Studio Catering,**

across from the studio tour entrance, near the corner of Mickey Avenue and New York Street, you'll find snacks.

BUYS **Under the Sea** is good for mermaid merchandise and movie memorabilia. Outside the Backstage Studio Tour behind Catastrophe Canyon, you'll hear the roar of the explosions as you shop at **Studio Showcase** for movie-theme gifts.

SUNSET BOULEVARD

TWILIGHT ZONE TOWER OF TERROR At around $95 million, this is the most expensive ride in the world. As the story goes, an elevator crash caused by a lightning storm in the 30s shut down the magnificent Hollywood Hotel. A Rod Serling double tells the story of an episode that never aired. Fascinating detail abounds, from the crumbling vine-covered exterior to the dusty, moldy interior, which is full of the TV show's most memorable props. A 13-story ride up is followed by a free-fall that includes a few seconds of actual weightlessness. Then, you immediately repeat the elevator ride and its sequel. The long wait is part of the experience.
Worth-It Rating: 5

BEAUTY AND THE BEAST STAGE SHOW This amazing production was so strong that it was successfully adapted for Broadway, where it is still playing to capacity.
Worth-It Rating: 5

BITES **Sunset Ranch Market** is a nifty bit of Disneyana, a re-creation of a place that Walt frequented in Anaheim around the time he bought the property for Disneyland. You eat outdoors on picnic tables; the fare is light, with lots of citrus specialties. **Rosie (the Riveters) Red Hot Dogs** is still more on the same theme. Legend has it that Walt used to stop at the original for a hot dog when he visited Anaheim. You can, too.

BUYS The **Anaheim Produce Company** recalls the orange grove that became Disneyland. You'll find citrus for sale. In the middle of Sunset Boulevard, **Once Upon a Time** features character merchandise from the classics. Near Hollywood Boulevard, **Legends of Hollywood** has books, posters, and videos of classic films. **Golden Age Souvenirs,** outside Superstar Television, sells goodies from the early days of TV. I got my Howdy Doody key chain here. At **Tower Hotel Gifts,** pick up a Serling for the den.

chapter 5

UNIVERSAL STUDIOS FLORIDA

The main entrance is on Kirkman Road, which intersects with International Drive at its north end. Take Exit 30B off I–4. Turn right onto Major Boulevard, the street that runs alongside the Twin Towers and the Mystery Fun House, directly opposite the park entrance. Make a legal U-turn and you will be pointed directly at the entrance. When the light turns green, drive right in.

Worth-It Rating: 5+
Subtract 1 if you're traveling with children under 6.

The best theme park in the world—that's what you'll hear me say over and over about Universal Studios Florida. The rides are the most spectacular, the shows the most thrilling. Each street scene has been in many movies. One of my family's favorite games is to try to recognize buildings and what movie we saw them in. If you overlook the little things, you'll miss a lot.

Remember, this park isn't the product of some second-rate outfit. Universal is the studio that releases Steven Spielberg films, one with a star-studded history dating from the Golden Age of Hollywood, back when Disney was just a cartoon factory. True, lines here can be painfully long and very hot, and the park has too much concrete and not enough green space and shade.

But despite that, and as great as the Disney parks are, I believe Universal Studios Florida is better than anything at Walt Disney World.

I use process of elimination.

The Magic Kingdom is a wonderful park. It was the original, and it's full of neat things to see and do. But it's still based on many concepts from the 1940s. It's dated.

Epcot Center is too much about shopping and eating and not enough about rides and shows.

Disney–MGM Studios is the newest and the best of the Disney parks. Since it's movie-based, like Universal, comparisons are easy. Both parks offer back lot tours that give you a behind-the-scenes look at how movies and TV shows are made. Both have first-class thrill rides and multimillion-dollar media productions available nowhere else on the planet.

Disney has Star Tours, an exciting ride based on George Lucas's *Star Wars*. Your simulator is a square room that shakes you and zooms you around in front of a screen that is even smaller than those in an average mall multiplex cinema. In contrast, Back to the Future has you in an eight-passenger replica of a DeLorean sports car that literally hangs you out in space in front of a nine-story IMAX screen. Star Tours is great, and my whole family loves it. But Back to the Future is about a gazillion times more exciting.

In no other theme park do you find the attention to detail that you do at Universal Studios Florida. For instance, Universal's rides not only look real, they smell real, from the salt tang in the air at the northeastern wharf outside Jaws to the scent of bananas on King Kong's breath at Kongfrontation.

As you read this chapter, you will see why ride for ride, show for show, this is my family's favorite park. The rides and shows are similar in structure from park to park: There are simulators and thrill rides, special effects and stunt shows, interactive film shows and robotics. However, in almost every case, Universal's version is bigger, more detailed, more powerfully presented, or just plain better. I give Disney the edge for cuteness and appeal to small children. But for kids old enough to appreciate the slimy goo at Nickelodeon and for the pure power of motion picture magic, sound, light, and spectacle, my envelope says the winner is Universal.

TIMING Because it is the best of all the parks, I recommend two days at Universal Studios Florida. And do it *before* you visit any of the Disney parks.

EATERTAINMENT Universal Studios has a bunch of decent munching stops. Reservations usually aren't necesssary but if you have your heart set on a specific place, book ahead. You can call up to 48 hours in advance; I give the numbers below, along with the descriptions.

SHOPPERTOONITIES Universal Studios Florida offers a number of unique shopping opportunities.

SHOWS & TAPINGS A schedule of shows is posted on a sign board near the entrance. You get a printed schedule when you buy your ticket. See my advice about attending tapings in Chapter 4. The number to call—do it before you leave home—is 407/363-8000.

THE LAY OF THE LAND Universal Studios Florida is laid out like a Hollywood back lot, with areas that simulate Hollywood and Beverly Hills, New York City and Chicago, and the wharfs of New England and San Francisco. Another area, Production Central, highlights the mechanics of show biz. Analagous to the Magic Kingdom's lands, these are arranged around a central lagoon.

THE FAST TRACK Most visitors bear right when they enter the park. Do what other people don't: bear left when you enter, and proceed clockwise around the park.

PRODUCTION CENTRAL

NICKELODEON STUDIOS TOUR According to recent A.C. Neilsen ratings, Nickelodeon is the number-one cable network. The line to tour the studios forms at the Slime Geyser, the giant fountain known to Nick fans that blasts green goo high into the Florida sky. Glassed-in catwalks above the sound stages give visitors a unique view of real TV shows in progress. Kids get to see how their favorite substances, gak and slime, are made, and may even get a taste! Game Lab, at the very end of the Nick tour, is like a fake game show with people in your tour group chosen to participate based on enthusiasm. (The kids and I know the drill, and one or more of us almost always get in.) The games are quintessential Nick—very physical and messy, ending with one lucky (?) kid getting slimed.
Worth-It Rating: 5. Minus 2 without kids.

FUNTASTIC WORLD OF HANNA-BARBERA This is the first ride you see in the park and the best ride for little kids anywhere. I wish Disney would do as well with Peter Pan. Bill and Joe (Hanna and Barbera) give you a quick look at computer animation. Then you enter a large simulator where you join Yogi Bear in a daring rescue of Elroy Jetson from the evil clutches of Dick Dastardly and his sniveling mutt, Muttley.
Worth-It Rating: 5

HITCHCOCK'S 3D THEATER I remember being scared to death in the early 60s, when Tippy Hedron was attacked in Alfred Hitchcock's *The Birds*. But that was long ago—maybe too long—and for most Gen-Xers, this show may be dated. The 3D is pretty neat, though: You'll almost want to check your clothes for droppings.
Worth-It Rating: 3

MURDER, SHE WROTE, MYSTERY THEATER For anyone who has never been inside a TV studio, this is an educational experience. Even for old TV pros, it's a lot of fun. The scenario is that the production of an episode in television's longest-running prime-time dramatic series is way behind, and you have to help the cast and crew. From filming to adding sound effects and voice-overs, you participate in the post-production.
The Fast Track: Act up and you could get a part.
Worth-It Rating: 4

BONE YARD Many visitors completely miss this not-necessarily-final resting place of props and gadgets from films gone by. That tarnished metal hulk once had the title role in *Jaws* and was as big a star as Richard Dreyfuss. Take a minute to stop and smell the rust.
Worth-It Rating: 5

EATERTAINMENT Hey, I'm a fat guy. So I know my buffets. **Studio Stars,** between Hollywood and New York, is one theme-park restaurant where you can get your money's worth! To reserve: 407/224–9530.

NEW YORK

SCREEN TEST HOME VIDEO ADVENTURE Let me warn you, there's an extra charge of $29.95 for this one. That said, we still cherish the *Star Trek* episode we taped five years ago. The whole family dresses up to tape a scene from *E.T., Back to the Future, King Kong,* or *Star Trek.* You're electronically inserted into the clip. Unsuspecting folks back home will believe you actually worked with the stars. I only wish it were a little cheaper.
Worth-It Rating: 4

KONGFRONTATION New York City's elevated rail line takes you face to face with the movies' biggest mechanical menace—Ol' Banana Breath!
The Fast Track: Beware of lines here—there's a lot more inside than you might guess. Go late in the day.
Worth-It Rating: 5

BLUES BROTHERS IN CHICAGO BOUND This show takes place in the street, in front of a reproduction of Jake and Elwood's walk-up from the movie. These guys are better than Akroyd and Belushi! Check your program for times.
Worth-It Rating: 5

BEETLEJUICE'S ROCK AND ROLL GRAVEYARD REVUE Rock & roll with the ungrateful dead in this loud, last-gasp blast from the passed with lots of bright and smoky pyrotechnics. Bring something to plug your ears.
Worth-It Rating: 4

BITES Remember *The Godfather*? **Louie's Italian Restaurant,** a Little Italy–style establishment, wasn't in the movie, but it could've been. Great pizza, of course. **Finnegan's Bar and**

Grill, an Irish pub where Universal staffers hang out after work, serves British beers along with hearty fare like shepherd's pie, live entertainment, and happy hours! Draw me a Guinness! To reserve: 407/363–8757.

SHOPS Doc's, on Delancey Street, is where the Blues Brothers shop. And you can outfit yourself in khaki and a pith helmet at **Safari Outfitters,** next to Kongfrontation. Or have your photo taken with the giant simian. Nearby is **Second Hand Rose.** Only Universal Studios has this kind of bargain basement full of its discontinued and discounted merchandise.

SAN FRANCISCO/AMITYVILLE

EARTHQUAKE: THE BIG ONE Charlton Heston narrates a behind-the-scenes look at the special effects for this classic film. Then you ride a subway into an 8.3 quake, complete with spectacular effects involving explosions and a lot of water. You might get wet.
The Fast Track: Act loud and crazy at the beginning and you could get picked to be an extra. Bring a camera.
Worth-It Rating: 4+

JAWS You are greeted with the unmistakable smell of an East Coast wharf, and then your boat is chased and attacked by a a terrifying shark. It took over four years for the Universal Studios engineers to get this thing to work. (In tests, the mechanical sharks actually sank the boats. Scary, huh?) The delay was worth it.
The Fast Track: Bring a plastic bag to hold anything you don't want to get wet.
Worth-It Rating: 5

WILD, WILD, WILD WEST STUNT SHOW This is a nifty look at how those shoot-'em-ups and blow-'em-ups are made. These daring stunt men are "real" men and almost as good as the stunt women.

The Fast Track: Bring ear plugs, especially for little kids.

Worth-It Rating: 4+

BITES The steaks and seafood at **Lombard's Landing** are not bad for a pricey theme-park restaurant. To reserve: 407/224–6400. Outside on the pier, a stand serves clam chowder in a bowl made of bread. Yum!

SHOPS Check out the wood and leather items at **Bayfront Crafts**, on the waterfront. **Quint's Nautical Treasures** sells *Jaws* merchandise. At **Salty's Sketches**, in Amityville, you can have a caricature drawn. Then there's **Shaiken's Souvenirs**, named for the fact that while you're shopping for San Francisco and Earthquake merchandise you can actually feel the earth quake.

Worth-It Rating: 4

BACK LOT

BACK TO THE FUTURE: THE RIDE I rate Back to the Future the number-one theme-park ride in the world. One of the greatest thrills of my career was when my wife and I attended its star-studded opening, along with Michael J. Fox, Mary Steenburgen, and Tom Wilson, who plays the ride's mischievous villain, Biff, who must be sent back to his own era, circa 1955. We rode nine times in a row! I also talked to Douglas Trumbull, the Hollywood special-effects wizard who designed this amazing ride, using the same simulator technology developed for NASA to replicate space-flight conditions.

The adventure begins in line as you are greeted by a research assistant from Doc Brown's Institute for Future Living. Pay close attention to the TV monitors—they're not up there just to help you pass the time. The presentation will bring you up to speed on your mission to capture Biff. Check the doorways along the halls for the names and memorabilia from visiting scientists such as Albert Einstein and Leonardo da Vinci.

Your simulator is a fake DeLorean, similar to the car that you saw in the film trilogy (the vehicle used in the movies is in front of the attraction). Once you're buckled up, a garage door opens to reveal the fact that you are suspended several stories up in front of one of the largest theater screens in the world, 90 feet high!

The Fast Track: The very best seat in the house is the center car on level five. Go ahead and ask the attendant for it. Occasionally, you can fast-track the left lane.

Worth-It Rating: 5+

BARNEY Too quickly, kids grow up. Sadly, mine are beyond Barney. Yours may still want to meet the famous purple dinosaur, Baby Bop, and pals at this live sing-along, play-along, audience participation outdoor show on a high-tech revolving stage. One highlight is an interactive outdoor play area where kids make music by touching glowing, singing rocks.

The Fast Track: Get there early so that you can sit up front. Remember that little kids are short and have trouble seeing over crowds. Check your schedule for showtimes.

Worth-It Rating: 5. Subtract 4 if you're over 5.

ANIMAL ACTORS STAGE Meet Lassie, Mister Ed, and many other four-legged stars. You won't believe that animals can do what they do here until you see them do it here, and then you may still not believe. Like many of the Orlando theme park experiences, this trained-animal show is the best of its kind in the entire world.
Worth-It Rating: 5

FIEVEL'S PLAYLAND Everyday household items are huge in Fievel Mouskewitz's land of the little. This world-class kids' playground has ball pits and moon walks, but its centerpiece is a water slide that will soak riders of any age. Nearby vendors and benches in the shade make this an ideal picnic spot, too.
The Fast Track: Plan to be on the Back Lot when the mid-afternoon heat is at its peak, around 2 or 3 PM. Then you can cool off and relax in this wet, shady, fun spot.
Worth-It Rating: 5

E.T. ADVENTURE This ride is a little tame, but it's an excellent look at how movies are made. The setting is a realistic re-creation of a Hollywood set, based on a forest full of topless concrete trees, filled with the props from the E.T. movie. You ride the bike with E.T. and see how many of the scenes and special effects were created.
The Fast Track: Long lines—get there early.
Worth-It Rating: 4

AT&T AT THE MOVIES Fans of AT&T will love this showcase of the role of America's largest phone company in films over the years. What, you've never gone to a movie to see AT&T?
Worth-It Rating: 3. Subtract 2 if you think your phone bill is too high.

BITES The **International Food Bazaar** is just like the food court at the mall, only better, with Italian, Greek, and American (among others). I like the killer desserts!

BUYS Just outside the world's greatest ride, you'll find **Back to the Future Gifts** and about a million different reproductions of the time-traveling DeLorean. You can also find your size in a Hill Valley High School class ring. Want to own the shower curtain from the most famous shower scene in history? Stop by the **Bates Motel Gift Shop.** Then there's **E.T.'s Toy Closet and Photo Spot,** with a zillion E.T. toys and a place to pose for pix with the famous alien. **Fievel's Playland Kiosk** sells Fievel toys.

HOLLYWOOD

GORY, GRUESOME & GROTESQUE HORROR MAKE-UP SHOW

This how-to demonstration on the making of Hollywood's grossest goo is only for the strong of stomach, liver, intestines, and other internal organs. In fact, you'll see all of the above entrails and then some at this festival of gore. Would it surprise you that many human body parts in the movies are actually made with real drippy, bloody meat and animal organs?
The Fast Track: Don't go at lunch time.
Worth-It Rating: 4. Subtract 3 if you are squeamish.

TERMINATOR 2: THE BATTLE ACROSS TIME, 3D When I

was growing up in the 50s, 3D film promoters predicted that exhibitors of the future would proffer their wares in special theaters showing only 3D movies. So far that has happened mainly at the theme parks. All their shows are worth seeing, but along with the number-one ride in the world, Back to the Future, Universal Studios Florida is also home to what I consider the number-one theme-park show in the world and the most spectacular production anywhere, Terminator 2: The Battle Across Time, 3D.

At the beginning of the ride, you enter the headquarters of CyberDyne Systems (frighteningly similar to Microsoft), where the future is being programmed. You are shown a wonderfully satirical film depicting all the amazing things that computers will soon be doing for you. Fans of the Terminator movies will already know what everyone else will soon understand: the machines are trying to take over the world. If Linda Hamilton can't stop them with the help of renegade terminator robot Arnold Schwarzenegger, humanity is doomed. Along with a 3D movie featuring Arnold, Linda, and other stars from the films, there are giant robots, incredibly realistic 3D effects, live actors on motorcycles, and incredibly fast-moving props zooming in and out of the screen, so that it's difficult to distinguish what's real and what's not. Audiences typically give this show a standing ovation. I went home and hugged my Apple computer.

The Fast Track: There are three opportunities to fast-track here. When you enter the building, the left lane may be open. Next, look for the place where the line changes to an assembly area; most people stay in line, so you can move ahead. Finally, in the holding lobby just before the theater, you can move directly to the area in front of the doors. Try not to sit in the front row. It's too close, and you don't see as much on the sides and in the back.

Worth-It Rating: 5+

LUCY: A TRIBUTE Anywhere else in the United States, this often-overlooked tribute to Lucille Ball would be a stand-alone attraction. From her awards to her gowns, this one-of-

a-kind collection of the personal effects of the Queen of Comedy is a must-see for her zillions of fans.
Worth-It Rating: 5

BACK LOT STUDIO TOUR Walk the sound stages, ride the tram, see the sets, and tour the Back Lot—but do it at the end of the day, when other people aren't. You can board the tram opposite Nickleodeon. You might just see a film in production. Big stars make movies here all the time (I've personally seen Steve Martin, Michael J. Fox, and a few others.) Don't miss the tour. That's what it's all about, after all.
Worth-It Rating: 5

BITES Schwab's Pharmacy recalls the soda fountain where 40s film star Lana Turner was discovered. You can discover overstuffed sandwiches and ice cream treats. **Mel's Drive-In,** the scene of George Lucas's classic, *American Graffiti,* is just like you remember. In **Café La Bamba,** they speak Tex-Mex. Try the yucca (it's a vegetable) or the ribs (Ricky loves 'em).

BUYS In the **Brown Derby Hat Shop,** you'll find every kind of hat. Remember Chevy Chase in *National Lampoon's Vacation*? **Bull's Gym & Sports Merchandise** is the place to get that Bullwinkle hat with the antlers you've always wanted. **Cyber Image-T2** Merchandise sells replicas of Arnold's zippered leather jacket and a special cut of the movie with some great scenes that were left out. The **Dark Room,** a "reel" old-fashioned film store, displays great black-and-white photos on the walls. The color film you can buy is strictly modern. So is the developing. Check out **It's a Wrap.** You can make yourself feel like Hollywood royalty, if you have enough money for its pricey 30s and 40s fashion. In **Movietime Portrait and Celebrity News,** you can step into vintage outfits and get your photo on the cover of *Variety* or some other rag.

Need a klieg lamp for the den? How about a plastic Oscar or a clap-board scene slate for your home videos? Stop at **Silver Screen Collectibles,** next to Alfred Hitchcock. In the **Universal Cartoon Store,** next to E.T., you'll find character toys and everything imaginable that relates to Universal Cartoons. **Universal Studios Store,** the biggest store in the park, has items from all the other themed shops plus Nickelodeon merchandise. In **Williams of Hollywood Photo Studio,** you pose in period-style costumes. In the Bone Yard, between New York and Hollywood, you'll find the dinosaurs—and **Jurassic Park Merchandise,** stocked with paraphernalia emblazoned with the logo of the world's most famous fictitious theme park.

THE SHOW AT THE END OF THE DAY

DYNAMITE NIGHTS STUNTACULAR Remember those great speed-boat chases on *Miami Vice?* They're performed nightly on the lagoon, in the middle of the park.
Worth-It Rating: 5

chapter 6

SEA WORLD

Take I–4. Eastbound, take Exit 27A, Sea World. Westbound, use Exit 28 (S.R. 528, the Bee-Line Expressway) and follow signs. The park can also be easily reached directly from the south end of I-Drive and from the I-Drive exit on the westbound Bee-Line.

Worth-It Rating: 5

Zoological parks have become somewhat controversial. The Free Willy theory is that it's cruel to keep animals captive. I take the opposite view. Attractions such as Sea World and Busch Gardens—both owned and operated by Anheuser-Busch—provide funding and expertise to protect many endangered animals. Every year Sea World responds to hundreds of calls for help, including many from state and federal authorities.

Sea World is a wonderful educational experience, and kids learn without being lectured. Knowledgeable staffers are on hand at every attraction. I am constantly amazed at the perception shown by even the smallest children at this wonderful real-life attraction.

TIMING Stay as long as you can—from opening to closing off season and around 12 hours when hours are extended. Because of how shows are timed, it's nearly impossible to see them all. If you do, you'll have no time left for exhibits. So set your priorities based on what interests *you*—there are no bad shows at Sea World.

THE FAST TRACK Except at the Wild Arctic, Sea World has few lines. Most people go to the right when they get here. My family goes the other direction, and I advise you to do the same. Here are some other tips:

- If you begin early, start in the back of the park and work forward. If you arrive late, start at the front. You'll get the best seats and views at shows.
- Near the entrance, pick up a computer printout with the day's shows; based on when you arrive, this recommends which shows to see.

THE LAY OF THE LAND Sea World attractions, exhibits, and shows are arranged around a small lagoon.

WHAT TO SEE

TROPICAL REEF This giant aquarium would be a stand-alone attraction anywhere but Orlando. Thousands of species of fish, coral, and anemones, most from the Caribbean, are precisely identified with little signs.
Worth-It Rating: 3

SEA WORLD THEATRE And now a word from our sponsor: "Window to the Sea," a once-over about the park's research, conservation, and breeding efforts. You'll also learn neat stuff about how dolphins use sonar. Later on, a show called "Water Fantasy" takes over the venue. Soothing music swells. Then,

before you, a fountain begins to glow with a thousand colors. It's amazing how they can train water to dance like that.
Worth-It Rating: 3+

DOLPHIN COMMUNITY POOL Newborn baby Flippers splash around in this nursery. My kids love it.
Worth-It Rating: 3

CARIBBEAN TIDE POOL Grab a surface scope (like a dive mask that you hold against the surface of the water to look through). You can see sea urchins, starfish, and anemones, and even handle them if you like. Cool pool!
Worth-It Rating: 4. Add 1 if you have kids.

WHALE AND DOLPHIN SHOW Trained humans run around the enormous Whale and Dolphin Stadium and fetch fish for these highly intelligent sea mammals performing the breath-taking leaps. Hundreds of whale hours have gone into teaching these two-legged land mammals to perform their tricks.
The Fast Track: One child is picked to be in the show. Get there extra early and beg, and it might be yours.
Worth-It Rating: 5

MANATEES, THE LAST GENERATION? Thanks to legislation championed by the folks here and by Florida's own Jimmy Buffett, these gentle sea cows are making a comeback. In this nifty environment, you can view them both above the water and beneath it.
Worth-It Rating: 5

KEY WEST AT SEA WORLD In this charming re-creation of Ernest Hemingway's Key West, you can learn the differences between porpoises and Atlantic bottle-nosed dolphins. At

designated times, you can buy smelts and toss them into the pool—smelly but fun.
Worth-It Rating: 5

SEA LION AND OTTER STADIUM The show here, "Hotel Clyde and Seamore," stars the Laurel and Hardy of the water, Clyde Otter and Seamore Sea Lion.
The Fast Track: You'll miss some of the best gags if you're too close to the stage or too far to either side. Go for the middle, half way back.
Worth-It Rating: 5

PACIFIC POINT PRESERVE An engineering marvel, this tidal pool is complete with the rocky Pacific coast and rolling waves. Here, you'll learn the differences between sea lions and seals, and get the chance to throw 'em a fish! (The fish is on you.)
Worth-It Rating: 4

PENGUIN ENCOUNTER Okay, pop quiz! What's the difference between a penguin and a puffin? Hint: there are no penguins at the North Pole. Both are here, in icy splendor. They're fast, they're funny, and they're all dressed up in black tie and tails.
Worth-It Rating: 4

TERRORS OF THE DEEP You stroll past a pool of live sharks into a theater to view a film on sharks, narrated by William (Captain Kirk) Shatner. Then, the screen rolls up and there they are, right in front of you in an enormous tank. But wait, there's more! Step onto a moving sidewalk and you are slowly propelled through an enormous plexiglass tube that goes right through the middle of the shark tank! Don't miss this one!
Worth-It Rating: 5

CLYDESDALE HAMLET Home of the world-famous Budweiser Clydesdales, the pride of Anheuser-Busch.
Worth-It Rating: 3

SHAMU WORLD FOCUS If you guessed that the Shamu Stadium is home of Shamu, you're right! In this show, you see the big guy on the big screen and in person with baby Shamu, too! It's four times the Shamu for four times the fun! At night, the show is "Shamu's Night Magic." Personally, I like Shamu best under the lights.
Worth-It Rating: 5

SHAMU CLOSE-UP Here's your chance to see Shamu's family up close and personal in the world's largest fish bowl (okay, mammal bowl).
Worth-It Rating: 5

SHAMU'S HAPPY HARBOR Imagine one of those McDonald's playplaces that's five stories high! This one-of-a-kind playground is complete with giant pirate ship and water cannons. And there's no waiting.
Worth-It Rating: 5

WILD ARCTIC First, you take a rough (a little *too* rough) simulator ride on a trip through the Arctic. Then you go through the world's largest walk-in freezer to view polar bears and other Arctic animals. The finale? A high-tech, interactive educational area.
Worth-It Rating: 4

ATLANTIS WATER SKI STADIUM The current show is "BayWatch at Sea World Water Adventure." Ricky, my son, calls it "Babe Watch!" It's a wild and funny stunt exhibition with lots of buffed bodies in spandex. After dark? There must be a law

that says that every theme park must have a fireworks show. "Mermaids, Myths, and Monsters," in the water ski stadium after dark, is Sea World's. Don't worry if it has a new name when you read this—the entertainment value never wavers.
Worth-It Rating: 4

ANHEUSER-BUSCH HOSPITALITY CENTER Free beer!
Worth-It Rating: 5

EATERTAINMENT

The big deal is the **Luau,** a Polynesian dinner show (*see* Chapter 13). The **Spinnaker Cafe** is where we get clam chowder in a bread bowl, a family favorite. At the **Treasure Isle Ice Cream Parlor,** also near the entrance, the specialty is the giant waffle cone. **Bimini Bay Cafe,** next to the Luau, serves mostly sandwiches and burgers but also has a good island-style chowder. **Buccaneer Smokehouse,** in front of the Sea World Theatre, and **Dockside Smokehouse,** next to Terrors of the Deep, are barbecue specialists. **Mama Stella's Italian Kitchen,** across from Penguin Encounter, serves pizza and pasta. At **Chicken 'N' Biscuit,** between the Sea World Theatre and the Sea Lion and Otter Stadium, I love the double chocolate cherry cake. At **Mango Joe's Cafe,** I always order the sizzling fajitas or seafood salad.

SHOPPERTOONITIES

If you want aquatic mementoes, Sea World is the place. **Shamu's Emporium, Shamu Souvenirs, Crosswalk, Outrig-**

ger, **Sand Castle Toys 'n' Treats, Coconut Bay Trader,** and **Stadium Gifts** all stock many items bearing pictures of Shamu. **Discovery Cove** has educational toys. **Ocean Treasures, Pearl Factory,** and **Wild Arctic** stock sea stuff. At **Cruz Kay Harbor,** you'll find that Hawaiian-print whatnot you've been wanting. Bunches of people buy Anheuser-Busch logo souvenirs at the **Label Stable, Gulf Breeze Trader,** and the **Gangway Gift Shop.** We love the frogs. Lots of places sell personalized souvenirs. Among them: **Kaman's Photo, Key Hole Photo,** and **Amazing Pictures** do novelty photos. You can have your face sketched at **Kaman's Artist** or painted at **Enjoy Your Face. The Ringcutter, Pearl Factory, Your Name in Gold,** and **Brewster Glassmith** make jewelry by hand.

chapter 7

THE SPACE COAST

The fastest route is the Beeline Expressway, S.R. 528 East. More scenic: Take I–4 East, then the East–West Expressway to S.R. 50. A safe and modern four-lane highway, it was the original route between Orlando and the coast and contains several authentic Florida attractions that I recommend.

One of the statistics that constantly amazes me is the enormous discrepancy between the number of people who plan to visit the Kennedy Space Center and the few who actually make it. It's a shame that so many people travel so far and get so close to the Space Center, only to miss it, one of the truly outstanding experiences in Central Florida.

Created at the height of the Cold War, it is surrounded by a large buffer area, a tropical wilderness that is one of the last places where you can see the Sunshine State the way it used to be. On the way in or out, we often stop to watch alligators sun themselves on the banks of roadside streams. If you leave early enough, you'll see the rose-colored dawn and a sunrise over the primeval wilderness just east of metropolitan Orlando. Plan an extra day and you can travel back in time to an original Florida settlement, take an airboat ride across the sawgrass, and see an authentic old reptile park, all within 50 miles of Orlando.

WHAT TO SEE

JOHN F. KENNEDY SPACE CENTER VISITOR CENTER I get goose bumps here. The impact of visiting the site of the greatest scientific achievements in the history of humanity simply cannot be overstated. Brave Americans first breached the stratosphere and shot to the moon from here, and still journey into space on a regular basis. It astonishes me that just an hour from my suburban neighborhood, I can see and touch the actual artifacts that transported all of us to the edge of reality.

In the actual NASA complex, the attraction is also Central Florida's best visitor value. The Visitor Center is free. Here, exhibits showcase everything that's been in space, from pressure suits to capsules that carried astronauts aloft. Don't miss the lunar landing module and the film shot on the moon—actual 16mm movies shot and narrated by astronauts on the moon. Outside, you can walk through the Space Shuttle Explorer, a full-size spacecraft. A Saturn rocket that propelled the Apollo flights—the largest rocket ever built—is displayed in a pavilion nearby. You view every inch of it.

There is a separate charge for IMAX films in four of the world's largest surround-screen theaters, with screens 50 feet high (five stories!). Some footage of these launch documentaries, shown nowhere else on earth, was shot in space by the astronauts using an ultra-high-resolution camera; some was taken from the Hubble telescope. One of these theaters shows its films in 3-D. Narration is by Walter Cronkite and Leonard Nimoy. Unless you're in training to be an astronaut, this is the closest you'll come to being in space.

At the Visitor Center, you can also depart for guided bus tours out to the launch pads to see the missiles that launched the Mercury, Gemini, and Apollo capsules, as well as those of the current shuttle program. (These also cost extra.)

What amazes me about the early space program is how low-tech it was. By current standards, we sent those people up in tin cans propelled by firecrackers. Close inspection of the rocket engines betrays pipes and fittings that could be at home on a plumber's truck and gizmos that display no more sophistication than my lawn mower. Many of today's luxury cars have more powerful on-board computers and navigation systems than Apollo used to go to the moon. One space capsule you can actually poke your head inside left the earth and returned controlled by nothing but row upon row of on-and-off toggle switches. I could literally spend hours standing and staring, trying to imagine the courage that our astronauts must have possessed to hurtle into the void at incredible speeds in those tiny flying buckets.

The Fast Track: Crowds can be very large, especially on launch days. Except on launch days, however, lines move pretty well. After you've walked through the Visitor Center, check the wait for the IMAX movies and the tour bus, and take whichever one looks shorter.

Launch days are another thing entirely. In peak season, roads may be so clogged that you can't even get near the place. The park may be closed, an admission charge levied, or special tickets required (which you must purchase in advance from the address below and pick up on the day before the launch in person, with photo ID). It's a lot of trouble, and the launch could still be scrubbed. Even so, I urge you to go if you can.

Bites: **The Lunch Pad** serves fast food. The **Orbit Restaurant** is a food court where you chow down on Italian food, southern fare, or cold sandwiches. **Mila's** reminds me of Florida the way it was when I came here. The food is like the food our moms used to fix. You'll find salisbury steak, ham with pineapple, Yankee pot roast, chicken pot pie. This place is neat! Other stands serve ice cream, pizza, and hot dogs.

S.R. 405, East Titusville, tel. 800/KSC–INFO in FL, 407/
452–2121. Open daily 9–6, usually longer in peak seasons. Bus
tours: $8, $5 children under 11, under 3 free. 3-D IMAX movie:
$6, $4 children under 11, under 3 free. Other IMAX movies: $5
per movie, $3 children under 11, under 3 free. Admission to com-
plex free except on launch days ($10 per person adults and chil-
dren 3 and up; purchase tickets in advance with a credit card at
407/452–2121, Extension 4343).
Worth-It Rating: 5+

U.S. ASTRONAUT HALL OF FAME One small step from the
gates of the Space Center is this attraction created by the
Mercury Seven Foundation, the original Mercury astronauts
and their families. The astronauts contri-buted momentos,
films, photos and artifacts to make this a worthwhile extension of the Space Center experience. Shuttle simulators provide realistic facsimiles of astronaut experiences. This is also
the home of the **U.S. Space Camp,** a summer camp that
gives children and adults the chance to train for space travel
on equipment used by early astronauts. It's the right stuff—
and the kids and I want to go, bad! *6225 Vectorspace Blvd.,*
Titusville, tel. 407/269–6100 (Hall of Fame) or 407/267–3184
(Space Camp). Open daily 9–5. $9.95 adults, $5.95 children
under 10, under 5 free.
Worth-It Rating: 5+

ON THE WAY

FORT CHRISTMAS COUNTY PARK This absolutely free
attraction, just off S.R. 50, is a genuine 19th-century Florida
settlement that grew up around a wooden fort built during
the Seminole wars. The fort's name, derived from its dedica-

tion on Christmas Day, makes the town's post office one of the country's busiest every December. Around Christmas, don't miss the historical reenactments. *23760 E. Colonial Dr., Christmas, tel. 407/568–5053. Open daily dawn–dusk. Free.*
Worth-It Rating: 5 (if you're nearby).

JUNGLE ADVENTURE Roadside wild-life parks like this were once Florida's main attractions. Most have closed. Some, like Gatorland, have grown modern and slick. Jungle Adventure is Cracker style, recalling the old backwoods types that used to roam, hunt, and homestead Florida's swamps and forests. It features about a zillion alligators, a petting zoo, and a small refuge for endangered species, including eagles and panthers. *26205 E. S.R. 50, Christmas, tel. 407/569–2885. Open daily 9–6. $9.75 adults, $7.50 children under 12 and senior citizens over 60, under 3 free.*
Worth-It Rating: 4 (but not worth a detour).

MIDWAY AIRBOAT RIDES Skim across the sawgrass in a high-speed airboat while spotting egrets, eagles, and other wildlife—perhaps even a gator or a water moccasin. Trips from Florida's oldest fish camp, on the Banana River, last 35 to 45 minutes. It's buggy and hot in summer, raw and windy in winter. *28501 E. S.R. 50, Christmas, tel. 407/568–6790. Open daily 9–4:45. $12 adults, $6 children under 12, under 2 free.*
Worth-It Rating: 5. Subtract 2 if swamps give you the creeps.

chapter 8

BUSCH GARDENS

Take I–4 west to Tampa, then I–75 north to Busch Boulevard or follow the signs. The park is about an hour and a half from Orlando.

Worth-It Rating: 4

It's a great park and a great deal, but you have to figure in the cost of the trip and the distance from Orlando. Add 1 if you're a true roller coaster or nature lover.

This 335-acre signature park from the brewers of the King of Beers is one of my family's favorites. The theme is a trip across Africa, with each area based on a different country; the park's ubiquitous German motifs are reminders of the Germans' colonization of the continent (and the German heritage of Busch beer). The roller coaster and thrill ride selection is second to none—and Busch Gardens is known for its world-ranked roller coasters. They're all modern with tubular steel tracks, different than the ones with tracks built on wooden scaffolding; the thrills come not from climbs and falls but from speeding through tight turns and hanging upside down. They are spectacular.

But the rides are only part of the show. The park's center, the part devoted to rides, shows, and exhibits, is surrounded by a huge nature facility made up of botanical gardens and a world-class zoological park. Many species roam freely across the African Veldt section. So take your time and be aware of your surroundings as you move from place to place. Some of the best experiences are neither rides nor exhibits but the zoo and the gardens.

EATERTAINMENT The food is among the best at any theme park, prices are reasonable, and the beer, which is stored, served, and chilled as only a master-brewer can, is as good as it gets. In some cases, it's also free!

SHOPPERTOONITIES Some of the park's best values are in the leather and brass shops of the Moroccan Bazaar. But Busch Gardens is also a great place to get safari and tropical style clothing as well as Anheuser-Busch logo gear.

THE LAY OF THE LAND Rides and attractions are in the center and the animal areas are around the perimeter. Lands include (moving clockwise from the main entrance at Morocco) Bird Gardens, Stanleyville, Congo, Timbuktu, Nairobi, and the Crown Colony.

THE FAST TRACK Be prepared to walk a lot. Like the real Africa, Busch Gardens is vast. Prepare to get wet. Two of the best rides, the Congo River Rapids and Stanley Falls, leave you soaked; put valuables in zippered plastic bags. More than any other park, Busch Gardens lends itself to my go-left strategy. All park guests enter through Morocco and flow naturally to the right. But if you bear hard left as you enter Morocco, you'll find a small walkway past the Hospitality House through the Bird Gardens. If you enter this way—the way that most people leave—you'll meet minimal crowds early in the day. You'll wind up in Egypt, where crowds will be much sparser than they would have been earlier.

MOROCCO

Don't miss the alligators, the musical performances, and the drills by the Mystic Sheiks Marching Band.

SULTAN'S TENT You'll know you've arrived when you see the scantily clad belly and snake dancers. It really is a tent—like a lot of attractions at Busch Gardens, this one is outdoors, right on the street.
Worth-It Rating: 4

MOROCCAN PALACE THEATER Back home, you could pay the full ticket price to see a world-class ice show like "Hollywood on Ice," presented here. It's a spectacularly costumed and choreographed tribute to the movies—climaxed, of course, by a Busby Berkeley number. The former figure skating champions who perform are dazzling (alas, no Tanya Harding).
Worth-It Rating: 5

BITES The **Zagora Café** and the adjacent **Boujad Bakery** serve huge pastries and wonderful coffees. Next door, an ice-cream shop dishes up giant waffle cones.

BUYS In the **Moroccan Bazaar**, leather and brass are hand-crafted before your eyes (and customized, if you like). Prices are great, especially on leather. More than once, I have traveled to Busch Gardens just to shop for it.

THE BIRD GARDENS

In the mid-60s, when I first started coming here, these beautifully landscaped gardens were the main attraction, along with the bird show and the brewery tour. Alas, I was not old enough for the free beer, which is now a favorite part of the park for many visitors. (And the brewery tour is gone now.)

BIRD SHOW THEATER After all these years, the hourly exotic bird show has changed little. Trainers interact with several species of parrots and other tropical birds and explain where each bird comes from and its markings, characteristics, and habits. The birds do a number of charming fetch-its.
Worth-It Rating: 4

ANHEUSER-BUSCH HOSPITALITY CENTER Free beer here! Plus pizza, sandwiches, snacks, live entertainment, and an excellent view of the park.

LAND OF THE DRAGONS

One of the best children's play areas anywhere, this land is a world of giant-sized children's tree houses, where kids can climb, explore, and slide.

DRAGON FLUME RIDE A delightful, kid-sized version of the park's trademark flume rides. Children who are under 56 inches can ride a dragon upstream and over the falls.
Worth-It Rating: 5

STANLEYVILLE

Don't miss the beautiful gardens of the Orchid Canyon and the spectacular view from the Tanganyika Tidal Wave.

TRANS-VELDT RAILROAD On the authentic narrow-gauge choo-choo that chugs its way around the park, you get the most extensive view of the African Veldt, if not necessarily the best. The train has the added advantage of providing transportation in the park, though not all stations are always open.
Worth-It Rating: 4

TANGANYIKA TIDAL WAVE The truth is that I liked Stanley Falls fine until I tried this bigger, better variation. The much larger ride vehicle at this splash-a-rama holds 24. And the ride is much longer, as is the 55-foot plunge, the equivalent of a fall from a six-story building.
Worth-It Rating: 5

STANLEY FALLS For many years, the definitive flume ride, with two to four passengers shooting the falls together in a floating log. Our family of four can all ride together, which is nice. But as theme park rides go, this one is a bit dated. It creaks a little, it's kind of slow, and the big drop is not as thrilling as the one on its newer cousin next door. But it does have character.
Worth-It Rating: 4

BITES Some of the park's best food is here. At the **Smokehouse** you find large portions of barbecued chicken and ribs. At the **Bazaar Café** the specialty is a generous barbecue sandwich.

CONGO

When you travel deep into the Congo, don't miss the view of **Claw Island,** home of Busch Gardens' majestic white tigers. There's also a **Trans-Veldt Railroad** station here.

THE PYTHON Busch Gardens' original steel coaster loops you over twice, but not totally upside down like the newer rides.
Worth-It Rating: 4

MONSTROUS MAMBA A high-speed Tilt-A-Whirl.
Worth-It Rating: 3

UBANGA-BANGA Good, old-fashioned bumper cars.
Worth-It Rating: 4

CONGO RIVER RAPIDS You ride with several strangers in a 10-passenger raft made from a monster truck tire, Florida's best water ride. Slide, bob, and float down the white water rapids to the strains of jungle adventure music. You may recall the story in Greek mythology in which Tantalus was to spend eternity with an unquenchable thirst, inches from water he could never reach. That's how you'll feel in the interminable line to ride. To keep cool, I soak my T-shirt. I know I'm going to be soaked when I get off, anyway.
Worth-It Rating: 5

KUMBA Two double-upside-down loops and 13 upside-down turnovers make this one of the country's longest and most exciting rides.
Worth-It Rating: 5

BITES The **Vivi Storehouse Restaurant,** between the Monstrous Mamba and Ubanga-banga, sells fast food.

TIMBUKTU

We call it Timbuk3 (as in, a little farther than Timbuk2), because by the time we get this far, we're ready for an eatertainment stop. And in addition to the amusements below, there's an excellent selection of rides for toddlers.

DOLPHIN THEATER The Anheuser-Busch guys own Sea World, so they put on a good dolphin show. It's amazing how they train these mammals to swim! They also jump, fetch, sing, dance, kiss the trainer, and eat raw fish.
Worth-It Rating: 4

MIDWAY AND ARCADE This is the best midway I've ever seen. You pay extra, but you win: We've won at least half a dozen lifesize stuffed animals here. It may be the only midway you ever visit where you feel that someone actually wants you to win something.
Worth-It Rating: 5

THE SCORPION If coasters are your thing, this single-loop thing is your coaster. You zip through all 360 degrees of the loop, hanging 100% upside down en route.
Worth-It Rating: 5

THE FESTHAUS Seat yourself next to total strangers at long wooden tables for lunch in this replica German beer hall the size of an aircraft hangar. German dancers, singers, and oompah specialists entertain, portions are generous, prices are reasonable, and the beer is the best.
Worth-It Rating: 5

NAIROBI

This is the place where your children can ride an elephant. Next door, you'll envy the Asian elephants on a hot day as they bathe in a cool waterfall. A petting zoo allows kids of the human kind to meet the animals they're named for—friendly, playful goats—along with other varieties of gentle farm animals. There's another station of the **Trans-Veldt Railroad,** too.

ANIMAL NURSERY TOUR There's always a new population of adorable babies here. You'll also see breeding experiments designed to bring back into the wild some animals that are now extinct, animals requiring special care, and baby critters just opening their eyes.
Worth-It Rating: 5

CURIOSITY CAVERNS Busch Gardens has turned the clock upside down in this habitat for nocturnal creatures. By leaving the lights on at night, they allow visitors a rare glimpse into the habits of several species of bats and nocturnal reptiles. In this informative presentation, you'll learn why bats may be the environmental answer to mosquito control, and Dad can play Batman.
Worth-It Rating: 3. Add 1 if bats don't give you the creeps.

MYOMBE RESERVE Just call this "gorillas in our midst." At this one-of-a-kind colony of African gorillas, glass walls offer the kind of views of these animals previously available only to Jane Goodall. With its educational audio-video narrative, this is easily worth a visit.
Worth-It Rating: 5

BITES The **Kenya Kanteen** is the area's fast-food stop, right next to the elephants and the petting zoo.

THE AFRICAN VELDT AND THE SERENGETI PLAIN

Busch Gardens' zoological park features literally thousands of species with over 40 on the National Wildlife Federations' endangered list. Lions and tigers and bears, oh my! You'll also find camels, giraffes, water buffalo, elephants, antelope, and more—it's a jungle out there! Three rides offer different views and tours.

THE MONORAIL By far the best way to see the animals is on this aerial adventure. The narration gives you details about the habitats and habits of every species along with occasional anecdotal stories, such as landmark births in captivity. We have taken both Tiffany, my daughter, and Ricky, my son, frequently since infancy, and I believe this park has sparked an intense interest in animals that will remain with them for the rest of their lives. Unlike the other rides that traverse the park, the monorail lets you off where you started.
Worth-It Rating: 5

SKYRIDE The skyride takes you over the Serengeti to Stanleyville, the center of all the thrills. It also offers an aerial overview of the whole park, spectacular for videos.
Worth-It Rating: 4. Subtract 1 if the line is too long, as it often is.

CROWN COLONY

We've already covered the monorail and skyride, each of which has a terminus here. But there's more.

QUESTOR Simulator rides are obligatory at theme parks (Star Tours at Disney–MGM, Back to the Future at Universal). Models and drawings in the waiting area of Busch Gardens depict a craft that recalls a late 17th-century Spanish galleon except that it flies. The ride simulates some kind of a future adventure in this craft—at breakneck speed.
Worth-It Rating: 4

CLYDESDALE HAMLET The magnificent Anheuser-Busch Clydesdales are on display along with their awards and memorabilia. Trainers are on hand to tell you about them.
Worth-It Rating: 3. Add 2 points if you have a true horse lover like our Tiffany in tow.

BITES The **Crown Colony House** is above the park with an excellent view of the veldt and rides; it's the park's fancy restaurant and has a wine list that's impressive for a theme park. The best deal we've found is on the excellent fried chicken, which the kids like a lot. Seating is first come, first served.

EGYPT

Behind Questor and the Crown Colony Restaurant, this is Busch Gardens' newest land.

SAND DIG Proving that Busch Gardens is among the most little-kid-friendly of theme parks, this simulated excavation lets tykes dig for buried treasure—plastic baubles that are theirs to keep as well as tokens redeem-able for bigger prizes.
Worth-It Rating: 5

KING TUT'S TOMB There's no curse on this reproduction of Tut's three-room tomb, spectacularly detailed right down to the burial chamber containing Tut's sarcophagus. It's a must-see, if only because everyone should visit their mummy.
Worth-It Rating: 5

MONTU This is an inverted coaster whose cars hang from the track rather than sit on top of it. Traveling at more than 60 miles per hour, it flips you topsy-turvy with a G-force of 3.85. It's the world's largest of this kind.
Worth-It Rating: 5

chapter 9

THE GRAND OLD FLORIDA ATTRACTIONS

can't say it too many times: You can't do everything. But a few of the vintage Florida landmarks are definitely worth seeing. Here are my top picks, with my favorites first.

SILVER SPRINGS In 1996 while we were all congratulating Disney on bringing the theme park to Central Florida 25 years ago, Silver Springs quietly celebrated its 100th birthday. Although it takes an hour and a half to get there, my family visits this 350-acre park at least once a year. It's built around crystal clear Mammoth Spring, the world's largest natural artesian spring formation and the source of Florida's awesome Silver River. Glass-bottom boat tours give you a perfect, time-less view of the dugout canoes on the bottom, where they went down before the arrival of Columbus. There are also concerts by big-name entertainers, a narrated cruise, and a four-wheel-drive trip through a dense cypress and live oak

forest. And, usually in summer, the springs is opened to swimming. Getting here brings you through Florida's magnificent horse country. It's just off I-75, a mile east of Ocala on S.R. 40. *5656 E. Silver Springs Blvd., Silver Springs, tel. 904/236-2121 or 800/234-7458. Open daily 9-5:30, longer during school vacations. $27.95 adults, $18.95 children under 10, under 3 free.*
Worth-It Rating: 5

GATORLAND Back when Owen Godwin founded the self-proclaimed Alligator Capital of the World, in 1949, Florida had dozens of alligator parks. But only Godwin had the foresight to put his just a few miles from a piece of land that later caught the eye of a Californian named Walt Disney. Today, alligators are literally on top of each other. There are three shows: **Gator Jumparoo** pits a hungry gator against a chicken in a leap for lunch (best in the morning, when the gators haven't eaten since supper). **Gator Wrestlin'**, an old Florida tradition, pits a full-size man against a man-size gator in an honest-to-goodness wrestling match. In **Snakes of Florida,** you'll see deadly Florida rattlesnakes, water moccasins, and coral snakes. You can ride an old-time choo-choo through Florida swampland. Or go for a walk in the same terrain. Back in the park, at **Pearl's Smokehouse,** you can actually see a man eating gator. Fried gator nuggets taste a lot like chicken. (Wouldn't you have guessed?) *14501 S. Orange Blossom Trail (S.R. 441), between Orlando and Kissimmee, tel. 407/855-5496 or 800/393-5297. Open daily 8-6. $11.95 adults, $8.95 children 3-9.*
Worth-It Rating: 4

CYPRESS GARDENS There are water ski shows at every theme park. This 200-acre complex of gardens, created in 1936 by Dick Pope, Sr., staged the first, and they are still world-class. Sparkling lakes and ancient cypress swamps surround the park, which is home to 8,000 varieties of plants and flowers from 90 different countries. You can tour the gardens on your own, with a guide, or on a scenic boat ride. Other attractions include the European circus acts, a Russian ice-skating revue, reptile and birds of prey shows, children's rides and games, and the spectacular Butterfly Conservatory. Don't miss the Southern Belles, the park's famed hostesses, who wear showy antebellum dresses. Just one question: How do they handle those huge hoops? *Off U.S. 27, about 22 mi south of I–4 between Orlando and Tampa, near Winter Haven, tel. 941/324–2111 or 800/237–4826; in FL, 800/282–2123. Open daily 9:30–5:30, longer in peak seasons. $29.50 adults, $19.50 children under 12, under 5 free.*

Worth-It Rating: 3

MARINELAND OF FLORIDA Would you believe that this is not only the original marine-life park but Florida's first movie park as well? Back in the 1920s, Cornelius Vanderbilt Whitney opened an underwater studio to provide stock footage for the fledgling motion picture industry. Public tours were an afterthought, inspired by Carl Laemmle's tour of California's Universal City Studios. The attraction has not kept pace. Still, it can be fun. It's on the East Coast's gorgeous ocean highway, between St. Augustine and Daytona. The adjacent Quality Inn is one of Florida's best undiscovered beach resorts—and a real bargain. *101 U.S. A1A, Marineland, tel. 800/824–4218. Open daily 9–5:30. $14.95 adults, $9.95 children 13–17, $7.95 children 3–12, under 3 free.*

Worth-It Rating: 3

chapter 10

WATER PARKS

n Central Florida you'll find more aquatic thrills than anywhere else on the planet. The Orlando area alone boasts five major water parks. At each, you'll find flumes, slides, pools, tubing courses, and kiddie areas. **Flumes** are tubular, curved slides greased with a trickle of water. **Water slides** are always open-sided and not as curvy as flumes. The key difference among them is the vertical drop, the number of feet between the highest and lowest elevations. You'll also find **tube courses,** where you float on a meandering stream. Most parks also have **wave pools,** simulating ocean action.

If you have small children, check the proximity of the kiddie and adult areas. If they're convenient to each other, it's easy for parents to trade off, one watching the small fry while the other enjoys the water.

TIPS AND BASICS Because free tubes are usually in short supply, rentals are available, along with lockers and towels. Also remember:

- Your best value is later in the day—after 3, 4, or 5 PM, depending on park, crowd, season, and weather—when temperatures drop, early sunburns thin the crowds, and some parks offer half-price admissions.
- Never, ever leave children unsupervised. Make sure that someone is watching each child at all times. Wave pools can be chaotic.
- Don't wear anything around your neck, wrist, or ankle—it could snag and cause serious injury. If you have long hair, pull it back, keep it tied up, and keep your head up when sliding!
- Use sunblock and watch your sun time.

ORLANDO AND KISSIMMEE WATER PARKS

WET 'N' WILD My pick for the best-value water park, this one on I-Drive is the original water thrill park and still offers more ride per buck than any other wetland. You'll find thrills in the giant wave pool and on the Bomb Bay and Der Stuka, both with 76-vertical-foot-drops; in the Black Hole, a slightly terrifying flume in the dark (not for the claustrophic); in the Bubba Tub, where your whole family rides together; and on the Fuji Flyer, a speeding downhill raft that seats four. This high-energy park is usually crowded from late morning until late afternoon. We always found the kiddie area inconveniently distant from the other rides, and the awkward layout forces you to do more walking than you'd like just to get to the individual rides' queue areas. *Exit 30A off I–4. 6200 Inter-*

national Dr. near Kirkman Rd., tel. 407/351–9453. Open daily 10–5, until 9 in summer. $23.95 adults, $18.95 children 3–9, under 3 free (½ price after 3, or after 5 in peak season).
Worth-It Rating: 5. Make that 5+ if you enter on the Universal/Sea World/Wet 'n' Wild Vacation Value Pass (*see* page 227); minus 1 if you have small children.

WATERMANIA This park opposite Disney's Celebration in Kissimmee duplicates most of I-Drive's Wet 'n' Wild but is generally less crowded. If you're staying on U.S. 192, there is no major benefit to traveling to another water park. And if you're water-parking with small children, it's worth the trip from I-Drive, because it's so much easier to supervise your kids in the two excellent small children's areas here than it is in their counterpart at Wet 'n' Wild. Plus, everything is right here: a giant wave pool, multiple flumes, several tube rides, high-vertical-drop slides, and a tubing course. The surfing attraction is one-of-a-kind; the action of the simulated ocean waves is so realistic that actual surfing competitions have been held here. Moreover, food and rental prices are usually better than in any other park. *Exit 25A off I–4. 6703 W. Irlo Bronson Memorial Hwy., tel. 407/396–4994. Open daily 11–5, with earlier openings and later closings in busy seasons and warm weather. $23.95 adults, $17.95 children 3–12, under 3 free (½ price after 3).*
Worth-It Rating: 4. Add 1 if you get a free ticket, if you're staying on U.S. 192, or if you have small children.

DISNEY WATER PARKS

Only Disney has successfully made water parks into total themed fantasy experiences, unduplicated anywhere. If that's what you're looking for, you will probably decide that the

Disney parks are worth the money. And if you're staying on Disney property and really want to do a water park, proximity and availability of Disney transportation make these parks an obvious choice. For ticket prices, *see* pages 227–229.

TYPHOON LAGOON The landmark of this attraction near Walt Disney World Village is a ship that was tossed atop a mountain during a terrible storm (or so the story goes). Forget the fact that there aren't even any hills here in Florida—this is Disney, where anything is possible. Highlights include the world's largest wave pool, a pair of incredible vertical slides (more than 50 feet high), three white-water raft rides, and a river ride, which takes you easily from place to place and to the well-equipped tykes' area called Ketchakiddie Creek. The unduplicated specialty of the house is a tropical snorkeling adventure where you actually swim with small live sharks (safely; I've done it, and I'm not brave. The hardest part for me was the icy water). *Exit 26B off I–4, tel. 407/560–4141. Open daily 10–5 (until 7 or later in summer).*
Worth-It Rating: 4. Add 1 if you're doing it on a Disney pass.

BLIZZARD BEACH Did I say Typhoon Lagoon's theme is far-fetched? Disney has abandoned all pretense of plausibility in this park. Here's the story: the weather turned freakish; a snowstorm blanketed Florida; Disney tried to cash in by building a ski resort; the sun returned; and Blizzard Beach was born. Mount Gushmore, at its center, is the source of multiple flumes. The high-vertical-drop slide is the world's tallest at 120 feet (12 stories). A radar unit clocks your descent on a big digital display at speeds of up to 60 miles per hour. The chairlift is a nice touch. So is Tike's Peak, a conveniently located, kid-size version of almost all the rest of the water park. At the Blizzard Beach Ski Patrol Training Camp, you can try to jump across floating simulated ice floes without falling in. The result looks sort of like *Baywatch* on ice. *Next to Disney All-Star Resorts. Exit 26B off I–4, tel. 407/560–3400. Open daily 10–5 (until 7 or later in summer).*

Worth-It Rating: 5. Make that 5+ if you're doing it on a Disney pass.

RIVER COUNTRY Disney billed the park as "a re-creation of the ol' swimmin' hole." It's a good one. While no longer Disney's premier water park or even a state-of-the-art water attraction by today's standards, it holds up well for what it is, a rip-roarin' chance to feel like Tom and Huck on the mighty Mississippy! And admission is lower than for other Disney water parks. Spreading out from its own sandy beach on the shore of a natural Florida lake, River Country has old-time rope swings, flumes, raft rides, and a smallish kiddie section (not particularly convenient by my standards). Water launches to River Country leave regularly from both the Magic Kingdom and Disney's Contemporary Resort. *Exit 26A off I–4 (follow signs to Fort Wilderness), tel. 407/824–2760. Open daily 10–5 (until 7 or later in summer).*

Worth-It Rating: 3. Add 1 if you're a Mark Twain fan.

chapter 11

DIVERSIONS AND ROADSIDE FUN!

Entrepreneurs from all over the world flock to Orlando in the belief that where there are millions of tourists, there are millions of dollars to go around. One company spent a small fortune on a theme park that would have featured a hotel designed to hover four feet above the ground, supported only by psychic energy. (I am not kidding.) Such places come and go pretty quickly. The few that survive are good enough to merit a mention, perhaps even a visit. I cover the best of them in this chapter, along with WDW destinations—like Disney Institute and Discovery Island—that are real alternatives to a day in the parks.

For the most part the little attractions fall into a handful of categories: go-kart tracks, fun houses, miniature golf courses, animal parks, and carnival rides. As an attractions connoisseur, I can tell you that some are better than others, but within categories the biggest difference is location. My advice? Don't waste gas driving to Kissimmee if you're staying on I-Drive.

Should you bother at all? With its huge pool of visitors, Central Florida has every kind of attraction that you have back home, and it's probably bigger, better, newer, and nicer here. But if you read my Chapter 1 and took the time to calculate your hourly vacation cost—even if you just use my hypothetical $33.57 per hour—you know that it's costing you at least $30 to $40 per waking hour just to be here. When you add that figure to the cost of, say, go-kart rides at $3 or more a lap, you are easily spending $50 to $60 an hour on go-karting.

Or look at it this way. If you can expect to see about one ride or show every 45 minutes in a theme park, a reasonable estimate, you can do about 16 rides during a 12-hour day. If a theme park ticket costs you around $40, the cost works out to $2.50 a ride. Some attractions are full-day experiences. Most, however, will set you back about $10 each, or 4 times as much as a single theme-park ride. To duplicate a theme park day, with its 16 adventures, you would be spending an average of $160 per person per day.

Obviously, you don't want to do that. However, if your family includes a real go-kart fan or miniature golf fanatic, don't let me stop you.

INSIDE WALT DISNEY WORLD

DISCOVERY ISLAND Walt Disney had a special place in his heart for this 11-acre attraction on an island across Bay Lake and the Seven Seas Lagoon from the Magic Kingdom. The island is now a zoological park accredited by the American Association of Zoological Parks and Aquariums. It is home to over 100 species of animals, many of them threatened with extinction. It is also the site of one of the world's largest walk-through aviaries. Also on the island are 250 species of plants and lots of tropical foliage. Featured shows include "Animal Encounters," the "Feathered Friends" parrot show, the "Birds of Prey" (eagles and falcons), and "Reptile Relations." Special nature programs are available; call 407/824–3784 for information. For ticket prices, see pages 227–229. **Worth-It Rating: 2.** Add 2 if you love nature.

DISNEY'S FANTASIA MINIATURE GOLF This is the biggest and best miniature golf course I've ever seen, a must-see for miniature golf enthusiasts. Enchanted broomsticks, dancing elephants, and other characters from *Fantasia* are the obstacles; fanfares from the film reward successful putts. It's next to the Swan and Dolphin hotels, near Epcot. *Buena Vista Dr., tel. 407/560–8760. $9 adults, $8 children 3–11. Open daily 10 AM–midnight.*
Worth-It Rating: 4

ELECTRICAL WATER PAGEANT On view several times a night all year long, this is like a floating version of SpectroMagic. You can watch it from the beach at the Polynesian Village Resort, where it starts nightly at about 9 PM. Then it moves to the Contemporary, the Grand Floridian, and Fort Wilderness. You can also see some of it from the Magic Kingdom's turnstiles area near the ferry and monorail. Ask at Guest Relations in City Hall for times. There's no charge.
Worth-It Rating: 4

INTERNATIONAL DRIVE AND ORLANDO

CONGO RIVER GOLF & EXPLORATION CO. A giant waterfall, fake mountains, and jungle props simulate high adventure at this minigolf course near Wet 'n' Wild. The humongous water-

falls feel cool even on hot days. There are tunnels, ramps, and rocks, and plaques tell stories at each hole. This one has a twin in Kissimmee. *6312 International Dr., tel. 407/352–0042. $6.50 for 18 holes, $9.50 for 36 holes, adults and children. Open daily 10 AM–11 PM.*
Worth-It Rating: 3

AIR ORLANDO Helicopter rides, for a price. *8990 International Dr., tel. 407/352–1753. $20–$395 adults, $20–$225 children under 12, under 2 free. Open Mon.–Sat. 10–8, Sun. noon–8.*
Worth-It Rating: 3

MALIBU GRAND PRIX In my opinion, these little race cars are a lot more fun and feel safer than the go-karts at the Kartworlds and Fun 'n' Wheels in Kissimmee and on I-Drive, nearby. *5901 American Way, Orlando, tel. 407/351–4132. $3.50 for license (includes 1 lap), $3.50 per additional lap for adults ($2.95 children 8–12). Open Mon.–Thurs. noon–10, Fri. noon–midnight, Sat. 10 AM–midnight, Sun. 10–10.*
Worth-It Rating: 2

ORLANDO SCIENCE CENTER AND LOCH HAVEN PARK Most big cities have a hands-on children's science museum. As you would expect in the city with neighbors like the Walt Disney Company, Lockheed-Martin, and NASA, Orlando's is terrific. It's enormous, with a planetarium and observatory on top, towering over Orlando's lovely old Loch Haven Park. Exhibits are always presented with lots of high-tech razzle-dazzle. The planetarium regularly has laser light shows.

Surrounding Loch Haven Park is also home to our art museum, which exhibits every kind of art from primitive to contemporary. The **Orlando Historical Museum** preserves our history, mostly that from the early part of this century. The **Central Florida Civic Theater** and **Children's Theater** are also here; shows change monthly. Loch Haven Park itself is a lovely, shady, lakeside preserve. This is the real Orlando, with an exotic mix of the Old South and big money. *Science Center: 810 E. Rollins St., Orlando, tel. 407/896–7151. $6.50 adults, $5.50 children under 11, under 3 free. Open Mon.–Thurs. and Sat. 9–5, Fri. 9–9, Sun. noon–5; Cosmic Concerts Fri. and Sat. 9, 10, 11, and midnight.*

Worth-It Rating: 5

PIRATE'S COVE ADVENTURE GOLF At this pirate-themed miniature golf layout, our favorite, the giant waterfalls are inexplicably full of blue food color. *8601 International Dr., Orlando, tel. 407/352–7378; Crossroads Center, I–4 Exit 27, Lake Buena Vista, tel. 407/827–1242. $6.50–$7 adults, $5.50–$6 children under 12, under 4 free. Open daily 9–11:30.*

Worth-It Rating: 3

RIPLEY'S BELIEVE IT OR NOT! One of the best photo ops in town, this building was intentionally designed to look like it's falling over. Inside you'll find oddities gathered by cartoonist Robert Ripley and his successors, including some weird stuff such as two-headed animals. When my son, Ricky, was six, he got so spooked that he ran out of the place. *8201 International Dr., near Sand Lake Rd., tel. 800/998–4418. $9.95 adults, $6.95 children under 12, under 4 free. Open daily 9–11.*

Worth-It Rating: 4

TRAINLAND TOY TRAIN MUSEUM This spectacular toy train display in Goodings Plaza includes one of the world's largest model railroad layouts. *8255 International Dr., tel. 407/363–9002. $6 adults, $4 children under 13, under 3 free. Open Mon.–Sat. 10–10, Sun. 10–6.*

Worth-It Rating: 4

TERROR ON CHURCH STREET This big haunted house in downtown Orlando near Church Streeet Station is full of things that go bump in the night. Are they live or are they memories? Most of it is in the dark, with black light. Teenagers love to take dates to scary places like this, so the folks at TOCS are wise enough to give teens a small price break. It all may be too intense for little kids. *135 S. Orange Ave., tel. 407/649–3327. $13 adults, $11 children under 17, under 3 free. Open daily 7 PM–midnight.*
Worth-It Rating: 3. Add 2 if you're visiting with teens.

AROUND KISSIMMEE

CONGO RIVER GOLF & EXPLORATION CO. A twin of the Congo River Golf on I-Drive (*see above*). It's 3 miles east of I–4. *4777 W. Irlo Bronson Memorial Hwy., tel. 407/396–6900. $6.50–$9.50, under 4 free. Open Sun.–Thurs. 10 AM–11 PM, Fri.–Sat. 10 AM–midnight.*
Worth-It Rating: 3

GREEN MEADOWS FARM This warm-and-fuzzy attraction, about 5 miles off of U.S. 192, combines a petting zoo and a tour of a working farm, with hayrides and cow-milking demonstrations. *1368 S. Poinciana Blvd., tel. 407/846–0770. $13 adults and children, under 2 free. Open daily 9:30–5; last tour at 4.*
Worth-It Rating: 4. Add 1 if you're bringing little city kids who've never had another chance to see a farm.

JUNGLELAND This animal park is neither as big as Gatorland, nor as funky as Titusville's Jungle Adventure. Skip it unless you're on a mission to compare all local alligator habi-

tats. *4580 W. Irlo Bronson Memorial Hwy., Kissimmee, tel. 407/ 396–1012. $9.95 adults, $6.95 children under 11, under 3 free. Open daily 9–6.*
Worth-It Rating: 2

MEDIEVAL LIFE Actors portray typical villagers in this re-creation of a medieval town, demonstrating falconry and crafts such as carving and weaving. Check out the dungeon and torture chamber. It's educational, fun, and free when you attend Medieval Times, the area's best dinner show. *4510 W. Irlo Bronson Memorial Hwy., Kissimmee, tel. 800/229–8300. $8 adults, $6 children under 12, under 3 free. Open daily 4:30–8.*
Worth-It Rating: 5. That's if you go after paying for Medieval Times. Subtract 2 if you pay separately.

MILLION DOLLAR MULLIGAN The claim at this golf attraction next to Old Town, which has a driving range, a nine-hole pitch-and-putt, and a nine-hole miniature golf course, is that you can win a million dollars. To do that, you have to make multiple holes-in-one. The odds are better in the state lottery—there, at least somebody wins. Despite the come-on, it's a good spot for duffers whose families won't allow them a whole day of golf. *2850 Florida Plaza Blvd., Kissimmee, tel. 407/396–8180. $4.50–$10 adults, $3.25–$6.50 children under 12. Open daily 8:30 AM–10 PM.*
Worth-It Rating: 2. Add 1 if you're a golf addict.

OLD TOWN A lot bigger than it looks from the street, this has always been a family favorite. The focal points are the park full of rides and the shopping, on a re-created brick main street, for mostly nostalgic items like posters from the 50s, old-time brand-name collectibles, etc. A nifty tropical store specializes in things for Jimmy Buffett fans. The kart track and arcade are excellent. And **Instant Ancestors,** where you dress up to have

antique-style photos taken, is one of the largest such operations in America. *5770 W. Irlo Bronson Memorial Hwy., Kissimmee, tel. 407/396–4888. General admission free; individual admissions vary. Open daily 10–noon.*
Worth-It Rating: 5

PAINTBALL WORLD If your vacation isn't complete without a paintball war in the Florida sun, don't miss this spot—the world's most famous paintball field, seen on ESPN's Annual International Paintball World Championships. In the games here, platoons of make-believe soldiers armed with real guns shoot at each other with exploding balls of red paint. Many families come to work out their aggressions. You can shoot your spouse here, legally! This is definitely not kid stuff (and in fact, children under 10 are not allowed to play). It's an excellent value and a unique experience. *Off U.S. 192 east, behind Old Town. 2701 Holiday Trail, tel. 407/396–4199. Pump gun $18.95, semiautomatic $25. 20-min games with 10-min breaks weekends 10–4 and on some weekdays in peak seasons.*
Worth-It Rating: 5

PIRATE'S ISLAND ADVENTURE GOLF Same as Congo River, above. *4330 W. Irlo Bronson Memorial Hwy., Kissimmee, tel. 407/396–4660. $5.50 adults, $4 children under 12, under 3 free. Open daily 9 AM–11 PM.*
Worth-It Rating: 3

RIVER ADVENTURE GOLF Yes, Virginia, there is another adventure golf with waterfalls (*see above*). *4535 W. Irlo Bronson Memorial Hwy., Kissimmee, tel. 407/396–4666. $6.42 adults, $5.35 children under 10, under 4 free. Open daily 9 AM–11 PM.*
Worth-It Rating: 2

TUPPERWARE WORLD HEADQUARTERS Okay, here it is, the world home of Tupperware. There's still big-name entertainment in the auditorium—we saw Big Bird. But the museum of food containers, alas, is closed and there are no more demonstrations of the famous burp-lock freshness seal. *14901 S. Orange Blossom Tr., north of Kissimmee, tel. 407/847–3111.*

chapter 12

SHOPPERTAINMENT

I n no other place in the world will you have more opportunities to buy more things bearing the likeness of Mickey Mouse. But there's a lot more to buy in Central Florida than that. So many people from abroad do major shopping here, in fact, that export specialists have sprung up, selling everything from Levis to electronics. Read on for some of my favorite shopping destinations—all open daily.

ONE OF A KIND

U.S. ASTRONAUT HALL OF FAME Know kids who have seen *Apollo 13* 13 times? Here at the main entrance to the Space Center, they'll find the best selection of space-related merchandise anywhere: patches, decals, and medallions from

every mission since Mercury; astronaut suits; model rockets; and more. *6225 Vectorspace Blvd., Titusville, tel. 407/269–6100.*
Worth-It Rating: 5

GATORLAND Yes, Gatorland. Although primarily known as an attraction, it is also one of the world's largest commercial alligator farms and sells great alligator shoes, boots, belts, wallets, and luggage at farm-direct prices. *14501 S. Orange Blossom Trail, Orlando, tel. 407/855–5496.*
Worth-It Rating: 5

RON JON SURF SHOP The world's largest surf shop, open around the clock, is a multiblock complex, announced by more billboards than even Universal Studios Florida. When you make the one-hour trek to Cocoa Beach, you'll find a three-story waterfall in the lobby, the world's largest selection of T-shirts, and surf gear, swimwear, exotic gifts, and a spectacular view of shuttle launches. *4151 N. Atlantic Ave., Cocoa Beach, tel. 407/799–8820.*
Worth-It Rating: 5

SHELL WORLD Who doesn't expect seashells in Florida? Here is the world's largest selection, along with loads of stuff made from shells. A shell-encrusted Volkswagen is out front. *4727 W. Irlo Bronson Memorial Hwy., Kissimmee, tel. 407/396–9000; 5684 International Dr., Orlando, tel. 407/3770–3344.*
Worth-It Rating: 5

SPORTS DOMINATOR I have regularly seen Reebok, Nike, and LA Gear shoes at this high-volume outlet for $9.95 a pair. It's not just a come-on. While I can't guarantee what they'll have when you arrive, I can promise you consistently amazing prices. Official uniforms of home teams everywhere also go for rock-bottom prices. *6464 International Dr., Orlan-*

do, tel. 407/354–2100; 8550 International Dr., Orlando, tel. 407/
345–0110; 7550 W. Irlo Bronson Memorial Hwy., Kissimmee, tel.
407/397–4700.
Worth-It Rating: 5

WORLD OF DENIM These two outlets are among the world's
largest dealers of Levis and casual wear. Volume keeps prices
phenomenally low, and many people come annually to stock
up. 1411 Sand Lake Rd., tel. 407/851–1773; 8255 International
Dr., tel. 407/345–0263.
Worth-It Rating: 5

DISCOUNT SOUVENIRS

Remember my rule: If you don't want to overpay, buy souvenirs anywhere but in the theme parks.

BARGAIN WORLD Originally just in Ponderosa restaurants,
Bargain Worlds are now some of the largest souvenir shops
around. You'll find a gazillion T-shirts, toys, and trinkets as
well as film, sunscreen lotion, sunglasses, and even jackets—
all at incredibly low prices. 6464 International Dr., Orlando,
tel. 407/351–0900; 8520 International Dr., Orlando, tel. 407/352–
0214; 7586 W. Irlo Bronson Memorial Hwy., Kissimmee, tel. 407/
239–7733; 5781 W. Irlo Bronson Memorial Hwy., Kissimmee, tel.
407/239–0077.
Worth-It Rating: 5

T-SHIRT KING If you promised everyone back home a souvenir and you want to get off cheap, make a beeline here.
Among many, many souvenir goodies, you'll usually find T-
shirts as low as five for $9.99. 2539 Old Vineland Rd., Kissim-

mee, tel. 407/396–8393; 5192 W. Irlo Bronson Memorial Hwy., Kissimmee, tel. 407/396–8874; 6362 International Dr., Orlando, tel. 407/351–0758; 5032 W. Irlo Bronson Memorial Hwy., Kissimmee, tel. 407/396–8122.
Worth-It Rating: 5

SHOPPING CENTERS, DISCOUNT MALLS

BELZ FACTORY OUTLET WORLD This enormous complex on I-Drive is two separate major malls with four smaller annexes. You'll find factory-direct outlets from top designers, including Etienne Aigner, Bally, Geoffrey Beene, Capezio, Anne Klein, Calvin Klein, and many more. Remember O.J. Simpson's famous Bruno Magli shoes? This is one of the few places you can get them, along with Reebok, Bass, Converse, and Stride-Rite; Levis, Jordache, and Guess jeans; Oshkosh B'Gosh and Polly Flinders children's wear; and home items by Fieldcrest/Cannon, Fitz & Floyd, Mikasa, and others. Toys, jewelry, cameras, electronics, luggage, books, records and tapes, fragrances, and many more categories are amply represented, and prices are up to 75% off retail. And you can buy theme-park necessities at rock-bottom prices at Everything's a Dollar, in Mall 1. *4949 International Dr., Orlando, tel. 407/352–7110.*
Worth-It Rating: 5

DISNEY VILLAGE MARKETPLACE Currently undergoing one of its frequent makeovers as a part of the new Downtown Disney concept, this offers probably the largest selection of Disneyana anywhere, and Disney trademark logos appear on everything from T-shirts to haute couture, from toys to treasures to sporting goods. While shopaholics search out the per-

fect Mickey golf balls, the rest of us rent the little sporty two-person boats known as Water Sprites. (You see them on many Disney waters, but this marina is the most convenient place to rent 'em if you're staying off-property.) You must be 14 to drive. And you can rent cane poles for angling off the dock—you'll catch shiners and maybe a bass. Hungry? Head for **Fulton's Crab House** (love those crab cakes) or the **Rainforest Cafe,** almost a theme park in itself; its enormous gift shop is filled with stuffed animals (all endangered in the wild) and environmentally p.c. T-shirts. *Exit 26B (Epcot) or 27 (S.R. 535, Buena Vista) off I-4, tel. 407/824–4321. Water Sprite rental: $13.50 per ½ hour. Canopy or float boat: $19 per ½ hour. Cane pole rental: $3.50 per ½ hour, including bait.*
Worth-It Rating: 2

FLORIDA MALL That this is the nearest major mall to the attractions is the only logical explanation for its standing as the area's number one shopping stop. Except that you can pick up lots of discount coupons here, it's probably nearly identical to your mall back home, with its couple of hundred chain merchants, anchored by Sears, JCPenney, Gayfers, Belk-Lindsay, Dillard's, and a new Saks Fifth Avenue. There's not a single notable specialty store with any local flavor. It's a good 20-minute drive from U.S. 192, and although it's just a couple of minutes from I-Drive, it's in an area you may want to avoid—the adult entertainment district to the north is home to most of Orlando's streetwalkers and their personal managers. *8001 S. Orange Blossom Tr., Orlando, tel. 407/851–6255.*
Worth-It Rating: 2

QUALITY OUTLET CENTER Although this mall is not as complete as Belz (*see above*), the Adidas, Florsheim, and Laura

Ashley here are the only ones in the area. *5437 International Dr. at Sand Lake Rd., Orlando, tel. 407/345–8676.*
Worth-It Rating: 4

FESTIVAL CENTERS

These are true shoppertainment—themed shopping centers where the entertainment value is high and the retail experience is offbeat and unique. Some have street entertainers or rides and activities for children. The main attraction is always the shops, usually one-of-a-kind stores where you're greeted personally by the independent individuals who own the business.

CHURCH STREET MARKET This is just across the courtyard from Church Street Station, and if you didn't know the politics of the place, you'd think it was part of the same complex. Actually, it was cleverly created by another developer to cash in on Church Street's popularity and its advertising. Still, it has a number of worthwhile shoppertoonities. If you've never been to a **Sharper Image** store, you can visit one here. It's an attraction in itself, stocked with whatever is the state of the art in virtual reality, personal digital assistants, or electronic doodads that work underwater. **Brookstone** sells fancy hardware. And, of course, there's food: The politically incorrect **Hooter's,** a sports bar, features spicy chicken wings served by scantily clad young women. And **Jungle Jim's** has family prices and a cute jungle theme the kids will love. *55 W. Church St., Orlando, tel. 407/872–3500.*
Worth-It Rating: 4. Deduct 1 if you have to make a special trip.

CHURCH STREET EXCHANGE This is the shopping part of Church Street Station, with over 50 specialty stores, many of them locally owned and operated. While **Historic Families** (the family crest store), **Old Town Magic Shop**, and **A Shop Called Mango** (tropical clothing) are duplicated at Old Town or the Mercado, there's enough here to warrant the trip. A flight-ready biplane hangs from the ceiling on the second floor, where there's also an excellent food court and **Commander Ragtime's Midway**, possibly Orlando's most extensive arcade, with about a zillion video games and claw machines. The fabulous **Buffalo Trading Company**, in the building that used to house Stanley Bumby's famous old hardware store, has all kinds of western items including copies of an autographed picture of Butch Cassidy and the Sundance Kid and many, many fringed buckskin jackets. The **Bumby Emporium**, also huge, sells Church Street souvenirs and lots of old-timey stuff. Out on the street, jugglers, magicians, bagpipers, and other musicians entertain day and night. *55 W. Church St., Orlando, tel. 407/872–3500.*
Worth-It Rating: 5

MERCADO The nearest shoppertainment complex to I-Drive, the Mediterranean-theme Mercado invites you to eat! shop! and party! The 60 festive shops probably include at least a few that are unduplicated in your experience. **Space 2000** has about the best stock of space souvenirs outside the Cape, and if your plans don't include a trip to the Space Center, a stop here is the next best thing. **Conch Republic** caters to parrot-heads (as fans of Florida's own Jimmy Buffett are known). You might want to check out one of my son Ricky's favorite spots, **U-Spy**, a whole store full of real, gee-whiz, honest-to-gosh, James Bond–type spy gear. Mercado is also home to **Blazing Pianos**, a nightclub featuring a trio of rock & rollers on dueling grand pianos. Talk about great balls of fire! Discount coupons, available at the Mercado information center, get you in for half the usual $10 cover. Mercado's strongest suit is its restaurants (*see* Chapter 13). *International Dr., Orlando, tel. 407/345–9337.*

Worth-It Rating: 5. Subtract 1 if you're not staying on I-Drive or if you're not eating.

OLD TOWN If you can imagine what an old-time American small town might have been like when the carnival was in town, you will get the feeling of this re-creation of a turn-of-the-century Florida main street, with over 70 one-of-a-kind stores. **Wound and Around** carries 45 r.p.m. records, along with other '50s kitsch. Want to redo your living room with that found-in-the-old-barn look? Check out the old metal signs and outdoor thermometers at the **Old Town General Store.** Want to emblazon a few things with your family crest? Visit **Historic Families.** At **Instant Ancestors,** cameras, costumes, and even the props used to take your picture are authentic. Old Town is also the home of the first Tilt-A-Whirl ever built, along with one of the oldest Ferris wheels in continous operation, the Big Eli, which dates from 1927. Old Town's developer found it rusting in an Indiana barn and had it transported to Florida piece by piece and reconstructed. Old Town also has the best go-kart track and video-game arcade in town as well as its own haunted house, similar in concept and execution (get it?) to Terror on Church Street. And the weekly **Saturday Night Cruise,** a parade of hundreds of antique cars, is nationally famous. *5770 W. Irlo Bronson Memorial Hwy., Kissimmee, tel. 407/396–1964.*

Worth-It Rating: 5

chapter 13

EATERTAINMENT!

All You Can Eat
(and Other Worth-It Meals
Around Town)

By now you know that I'm very focused on value. And for value in dining, it's hard to beat all-you-can-eat buffets. But watch out! Some real stinkers flourish on the heartburn of unsuspecting tourists—after all, with more than 40 million visitors in the area each year, who needs repeat business. Here are a few that will leave you sated, not sorry, plus a few other not-to-miss mealtime opportunities. Children under 3 are often free.

BEST BREAKFASTS AND BRUNCHES

At Sunday brunches, champagne flows freely.

ANGEL'S DINER Check out this 50s-style restaurant. You'll be served hot breakfast items until you stop asking for more.

And the price is reasonable—the average breakfast check is $5 to $10. *304 W. Colonial Dr., tel. 407/426–2029, and 7220 S. Orange Blossom Tr., tel. 407/856–1968, both in Orlando; 7300 W. Irlo Bronson Memorial Hwy., Kissimmee, tel. 407/397–1960.*
Worth-It Rating: 5

DISNEY CHARACTER BREAKFASTS These events in WDW hotels and theme park restaurants give you and your kids direct contact with your favorite characters for photos, autographs, and treasured memories. If the one you attend is in a theme park, you are admitted before the park opens to the public, when it is nearly empty. The magnificent landscaping is at its best and most beautiful, as the cast members ready the grounds for the new day. Plan on around $15 per adult and $8 per child 11 and under. Reserve via 407/WDW–DINE as early as possible (up to 60 days in advance).
Worth-It Rating: 5

SUNDAY BRUNCH AT THE LANGFORD For the area's best affordable Sunday brunch, drive to Winter Park's Langford Resort Hotel, a grand old European-style resort in a shady corner of Central Florida's most prestigious community. No two weeks' buffets are quite the same, but the selection is always excellent and the quality is renowned. *300 E. New England Ave., Winter Park, tel. 407/644–3400. $15.95 adults, $7.95 children.*
Worth-It Rating: 5

SUNDAY BRUNCH AT THE RENAISSANCE ORLANDO The 150 items on the buffet at this resort next to Sea World, at the southern end of I-Drive, vary slightly week to week but may include—as on our latest visit—succulent lamb, perfect eggs

Benedict, and much more. *6677 Sea Harbor Dr., Orlando, tel. 407/351–5555, or 800/327–6677. $29.95 adults, $14.95 children.*
Worth-It Rating: 5

CELEBRITY THEME RESTAURANTS

HARD ROCK CAFE Orlando's version of the house that rocks is shaped like a giant guitar. You walk down the neck and take a seat in the guitar's body to dine from a menu featuring mostly soup, salad, and sandwiches. Pig sandwiches are a specialty—a hefty portion of pulled pork with barbecue sauce on a bun with cole slaw and fries. Prices are moderate, in the $10 range. You'll also find loud rock music, memorabilia, and zillions of T-shirts with the famous "Save The Planet" logo. *5800 Kirkman Rd., Orlando, tel. 407/351–7625.*
Worth-It Rating: 5

PLANET HOLLYWOOD A giant illuminated globe that looks like it fell from the roof of Superman's Daily Planet dominates the skyline of Downtown Disney. Inside, celebrity owners Arnold Schwarzenegger, Sly Stallone, Bruce Willis, and Demi Moore have stuffed four levels with more movie stuff than you could ever imagine. Prices are higher than they should be; skip the ribs. *Downtown Disney, Lake Buena Vista, tel. 407/827–7827.*
Worth-It Rating: 3

RACE ROCK The latest celebrity theme restaurant—my pick as the best deal of the breed—is from stock car king Richard Petty, Indy racer Michael Andretti, and several of their fast friends. You're served by uniformed trophy babes and pit

crew under awesome race cars and boats, suspended from the ceiling; you'll find loads of racing memorabilia and race car simulators, too. But the highlight is the food, mainly mildly spicy Tex-Mex with some great barbecue. In the lobby, an open-sided tractor-trailer sells all kinds of racing-logo souvenirs. *8986 International Dr., Orlando, tel. 407/248–9876.*
Worth-It Rating: 5

FAMILY BUFFETS—MY TOP PICKS

A number of theme-park restaurants offer all-you-can-eat buffets; I've included them in my write-ups of the specific parks. In addition to the Ponderosa steak houses—extremely clean and well-run in Orlando—a number of other chains offer other all-you-can-eat family meals.

GOLDEN CORRAL This is by far the most ample and best-run family buffet in town. Entrées generally include several varieties of chicken and carved turkey, ham, and/or roast beef. A bountiful salad bar sits next to a side bar full of steaming soups and vegetables. Yum! Especially at these prices. *7251 W. Colonial Dr., tel. 407/297–1920; 8032 International Dr., tel. 407/352–6606, both in Orlando. $5.49 adults ($6.49 after 4 PM), $3.49 children.*
Worth-It Rating: 5

SIZZLING WOK A stuff-yourself Chinese buffet with lots of tasty Cantonese, Mandarin, and Hunan entrées along with a do-it-yourself Mongolian barbecue. When we were last there, the salad bar was loaded with cold shrimp. The Florida Mall area, where this is located, is about 20 minutes from Lake

Buena Vista. *1453 Sand Lake Rd., Orlando, tel. 407/438–8389. Adults $4.95 at lunch, $8.99 at dinner; children $3.25 and $4.99.* **Worth-It Rating: 4**

DINNER THEATERS

These spectacular productions cost literally millions of dollars to produce. Beer and wine are served.

AMERICAN GLADIATORS ORLANDO–LIVE The live version of the famous TV show is 90 minutes of stunts, grunts, and battling hard-bodies in skin-tight spandex. The food is okay and the show is a lot of fun if a little pricey. *55 W. Irlo Bronson Memorial Hwy., Kissimmee, tel. 800/BATTLE4US or 407/390–0000. Shows nightly at 7:30. $34.95 adults, $21.50 children 3–12.*
Worth-It Rating: 3

ARABIAN NIGHTS Featuring the self-proclaimed "world's greatest thrill riders," this show is spectacular, especially for horse lovers. Too bad—the prime-rib is sub-par. *6225 W. Irlo Bronson Memorial Hwy., Kissimmee, tel. 800/553–6116. Shows nightly at 7:30 (two shows nightly in peak seasons). $36.95 adults, $24.95 children 2–11.*
Worth-It Rating: 3

CAPONE'S You have to know the password to get into this speakeasy featuring a Runyonesque musical comedy set in gangland Chicago in the 1930s. What the food may lack in quality, the buffet more than makes up in quantity. Costumed and in character, the servers keep the hooch coming. *4740 W.*

Irlo Bronson Memorial Hwy., Kissimmee, tel. 407/397–2378. Shows nightly at 7:30. $31.99 adults, $16.99 children 3–12.
Worth-It Rating: 4

HOOP DEE DOO REVUE The long-running Wild West musical revue in WDW's Fort Wilderness features frontier guys and gals in gingham, jeans, and buckskin singing, dancing, and pratfalling their way into your heart. Small children think the slapstick's hilarious, and it's hard not to have a good time. Plus, the chicken, ribs and country fixins are downright good! *Fort Wilderness Campground Resort, Walt Disney World, tel. 407/WDW–DINE. Shows nightly at 5, 7:15, and 9:30. $37 adults, $19.50 children 3–11.*
Worth-It Rating: 4

KING HENRY'S FEAST Jesters, jugglers, acrobats, and magicians are all on hand. However, unless you're going to do two medieval dinner shows, or you've already seen Medieval Times, skip this one. *8984 International Dr., Orlando, tel. 407/351–5151. Shows nightly at 7 or 9:30. $34.95 adults, $21.95 children 3–11.*
Worth-It Rating: 4

LUAU AT SEA WORLD OF FLORIDA This exploitation of a Disney concept scores no points for originality. Still, it costs less. And if Disney's is booked, this one is a good bet, with singers, musicians, and dancers doing the hula and the fire dance. *7007 Sea World Dr., Orlando, tel. 407/363–2559. Shows nightly at 6:15. $29.95 adults, $19.95 children 8–12, $9.95 children 3–7.*
Worth-It Rating: 4

MEDIEVAL TIMES My favorite dinner show is also the area's most successful, a re-creation of a joust and tournament com-

plete with knights on horseback, sword fights, falconry, and more—all performed while you feast. The food is better than competitors', the pageantry majestic, and the plot romantic; the trained animals are amazing and the fights exciting and realistic. There is truly something for everyone. Though my family goes often, we always enjoy the show; it's always slightly different and seems better than the time before. It sells out early, so reserve well ahead. *U.S. 192 at U.S. 441, Orlando, tel. 800/229–8300. Shows nightly at 8 (8 and 10 in peak seasons). $34.95 adults, $22.95 children 3–12.*
Worth-It Rating: 5

MURDER WATCH MYSTERY DINNER THEATER You'll have to be good to figure out "whodunit" at this show at the Grosvenor Hotel, a real killer! And the food is excellent. It's only on Saturday night. *1850 Hotel Plaza Blvd., Lake Buena Vista, tel. 407/827–6500, ext. 6103. Shows at 6 and 9, Saturday only. $33.95 adults, $18.95 children 9 and under.*
Worth-It Rating: 5

PIRATES DINNER ADVENTURE A life-size pirate ship sails seas of real water in the center of the cavernous arena that houses this huge production just off I-Drive. Circus acrobats swing overhead as you swig beer and sangria. Very entertaining. *6400 Carrier Dr., Orlando, tel. 800/866–AHOY or 407/248–0590. Shows Tues.–Sun. at 6:30. $33.95 adults, $19.95 children 3–11.*
Worth-It Rating: 4

POLYNESIAN LUAU South Seas islanders perform the hula, the fire dance, and other feats while you feast on roast pork, poi, and other delicacies. Known worldwide as one of WDW's trademark events, it will always hold up. Reserve way ahead. *Polynesian Village Resort, Walt Disney World, tel.*

407/WDW–DINE. Shows daily at 4:30 and 6:45. $37 adults, $19.50 children 3–11.
Worth-It Rating: 4

WILD BILL'S In this redo of Buffalo Bill's Wild West Show, you'll thrill to horse-riding, Native American dancing, western dancing, sharpshooting, knife throwing, rope tossing and just plain general hoopla! *5260 W. Irlo Bronson Memorial Hwy., Kissimmee, tel. 407/351–5151. Shows nightly at 7 (sometimes also at 9:30). $33.95 adults, $19.95 children 3–11.*
Worth-It Rating: 4

LOBSTER FEASTS

All-you-can-eat lobster dinners may sound too good to be true, but there are (count 'em) two in the attractions area plus one great seafood lunch buffet.

ANGEL'S LOBSTER FEAST Although this one at the Holiday Inn Main Gate isn't quite up to Boston Lobster Feast (*see below*), with fewer entrées, it comes close! *7300 W. Irlo Bronson Memorial Hwy., Kissimmee, tel. 407/397–1960. Lobster buffet $19.95 adults and children, $5.95 for children under 12 without lobster.*
Worth-It Rating: 4

BOSTON LOBSTER FEAST This is the best! It is also my favorite buffet anywhere! All-you-can-eat steamed lobster with hot butter is the Maine attraction along with crab, shrimp, oysters, clams, and fresh fish. I love the calamari salad, the lobster bisque, and the New England clam chowder. For landlubbers, they even serve a tender London broil.

And the price is just fine. *8204 Crystal Clear Ln., near the Florida Mall, Orlando, tel. 407/438–0607. $24.95 adults, $15.95 children under 12. No reservations.*
Worth-It Rating: 5

CRAB HOUSE Stuff yourself on crab, shrimp, and shellfish here. At dinner, there's a good selection of straightforward seafood entrées as well. *8496 Palm Parkway, tel. 407/239–1888, and 8291 International Dr., tel. 407/352–6140, both in Orlando. Buffets $9.99 at lunch, $17.99 at dinner for all. No reservations.*
Worth-It Rating: 4

SUSHI AND THE SOUTH SEAS

KOBE JAPANESE STEAK HOUSE I'm a regular at the two locations of this local chain that still offer regular all-you-can-eat sushi nights. The sushi is all hand-made to your order. Call ahead to check dates. You'll also find the area's best teppanyaki restaurant, featuring a dazzling samurai chef at every table. And the price is right. The Colonial Drive location is at least 30 minutes from U.S. 192, at least 20 minutes from I-Drive. The Altamonte Springs location is just off I–4, 15 minutes from U.S. 192, 10 minutes from I-Drive. *2110 E. Colonial Dr., Orlando, tel. 407/895–6868; 468 W. S.R. 436, Altamonte Springs, tel. 407/862–2888. $18.95 for all.*
Worth-It Rating: 4

OHANA Though the pay-one-price meal that goes with this show at Disney's Polynesian Village Resort is not officially all-you-can-eat, nobody ever refused us seconds. I kept ordering more of the super-jumbo skewered-and-grilled shrimp. You get a Polynesian name and a chance to participate in the

show. It's great fun and great food, both at an appealing price. *Polynesian Village Resort, Walt Disney World, tel. 407/939–3463. $19.95 adults, $14.95 children 12–16, $8.95 children 3–11.*
Worth-It Rating: 5

MY OTHER FAVORITE MEAL SPOTS

IN DISNEY VILLAGE MARKETPLACE I like a couple of places here. **Fulton's Crab House,** in the big paddle wheeler halfway between the Marketplace and Pleasure Island, serves fresh seafood—and lots of crab. The **Rainforest Cafe,** whose smoldering volcano towers over the area, is almost a theme park in itself, a jungle scattered with robotic animals. The menu includes burgers, sandwiches, salads, and, in a nod to the theme, tropical drinks. If there's a long line for the restaurant, head for the bar. *Call 407/WDW–DINE for all WDW reservations.*

FABULOUS BUBBLE ROOM Here it's always Howdy Doody time; every table is a display case crammed with toys from your childhood (Hopalong Cassidy lunch boxes, etc.). The prime rib is the biggest I've seen outside of Omaha. Rich, rich, rich red velvet cake is my favorite dessert. One of a kind. *1351 S. Orlando Ave. (U.S. 17/92), Maitland, tel. 407/628–3331. Average dinner check $14–$27.*
Worth-It Rating: 5

IN THE MERCADO We like a few eating spots in this Lake Buena Vista shopping-and-dining center. **Bergamo's** (tel. 407/352–3805) serves a tasty seafood linguine for $24.95 among other entrées. Singers entertain you with an Italian-American repertoire that includes plenty of Sinatra favorites.

At **Charlie's Lobster House** (tel. 407/352–6929), you find simply seafood, simply prepared, plus truly excellent Maryland crab cakes for around $18.95. And at **Butcher Shop** (tel. 407/363–9727), you can pick your steak ($16.95 and up) and either cook it yourself at the open grill or have the chefs grill it for you. At **Blazing Pianos** (tel. 407/363–5104), a good bet after dinner, pianists try to outdo each other with keyboard pyrotechnics on no fewer than three bright red pianos.
Worth-It Rating: 4

MICKEY D'S If you have a young child, you know how hard it is to pass a McDonald's without going in. You can imagine how hard it is to pass Mickey D's, the world's largest McDonald's! Fifty-foot-high fries mark a facility so sprawling that you need an elevator to get you to the PlayPlace, which is also the world's largest. You'll also find a theater, an ice cream parlor, a huge arcade with several simulators and over 50 other games, and a Know Before You Go discount hotel and ticket broker. Merchandise in the expansive gift shop reads "You gotta see this place!" You do, indeed. *2430 Sand Lake Rd. at International Dr., Orlando, tel. 407/859–7123.*
Worth-It Rating: 5

chapter 14

WHERE TO STAY

entral Florida residents often claim that a state law requires each household to offer free accommodations to all friends, relatives, acquaintances, and acquaintances of acquaintances who pass through town. That's just a joke. But the situation is the same, despite the 80,000 hotel rooms around town (more than in any other city in the world) and despite the rock-bottom-budget prices of many of them.

Since our family already has our quota of visiting out-of-towners, I'm going to give you the next best thing—the very best hotel values around town. First I'll give you my short list, my absolute personal favorites. Then I'll give you a range of other good bets for each of the several major lodging areas. I list all my picks with the least expensive first. Why do you need my recommendations? When I started Visitor Information Television, I called on nearly every hotel and motel in the area to try to get them to carry our channel. I have visited every one of the properties listed here again and again over the years. Hopefully, as a result, I know a few things that you don't, such as:

- Florida swamps breed mosquitoes the size of butterflies and cockroaches the size of golf balls. If your motel was built over a swamp, as many properties were, the only way to keep the bugs under control is with chemicals. I have been in rooms that made my nose burn and my eyes turn blood red. (I left those places off the list.)
- Some tourist traps are seedy, sleazy and just plain dirty. *They* won't tell you just how bad they are when you check in.
- Most resorts advertise in the local tourist publications. Many post rates daily on electric signs. Because I live and work here, I read the same publications and see the same signs you do—but all the time. I include the places that regularly post the lowest rates and deliver the best value in each area, in each price category.

Not every place that didn't make my list is a flea bag or a toxic dump. Some were omitted just because I don't know them personally, others because I didn't think they delivered value equal to their rates. I've picked the best in each price category in each area; good properties like the Grand Floridian— not a personal favorite but a perfectly fine place—aren't included. The ones I did include I can recommend without reservation. Information about the facilities follows my comments. Unless I tell you otherwise, all properties have video games, at least one swimming pool, a no-pets-allowed policy, and transportation to and from some major area attractions (noted below when it's free).

WHERE TO STAY

PRICE CATEGORIES Dollar-sign symbols indicate regular nightly rates for two people in a room (called rack rates in the hospitality industry):

Budget	$	under $45
Moderate	$$	$45–$89
Upscale	$$$	$90 and up

MAIN ATTRACTIONS AREAS Hotels in and around Orlando are clustered in three main areas:

Lake Buena Vista: This area contains Walt Disney World, Downtown Disney, Disney Village Marketplace, and Pleasure Island and is convenient to Disney attractions. Unless otherwise noted, to reserve at hotels on Disney property, contact WDW Central Reservations (Box 10100, Lake Buena Vista, FL 32830, tel. 407/934–7639 or407/824–3000).

International Drive: Universal Studios Florida is on the north end of this busy strip, Sea World on the south. It's also home to the Orlando Convention Center, Wet 'n' Wild, and several smaller attractions. There are more rooms and places to eat here than in any other area.

U.S. 192 corridor in Kissimmee: A.k.a. Irlo Bronson Memorial Highway, the strip begins at the end of Disney property near the Magic Kingdom and Celebration, the new Disney planned community. It is close to Watermania, Medieval Times, Old Town, Wild Bill's, and other sites. This is also where you'll find some of the area's lowest room rates. Parts of the area are also known as Maingate, because this used to be the main gate to the Magic Kingdom when the Magic Kingdom was all there was to Walt Disney World. In downtown Kissimmee, U.S. 192 is also known as Vine Street. Most of the time, it reminds me of a Hollywood movie set, all front with no back. Kissimmee/Osceola County is one of

America's largest cattle-producing areas. Check it out: Just a few feet behind the strip, cows still graze.

If you choose hotels that I haven't recommended, always get the exact location (or look it up on a map). And don't be misled by names. Some properties add the name of an area to its own (i.e. Maingate, Lake Buena Vista). For instance, several hotels that have called themselves Orlando North (not on my list) are really in Maitland and Altamonte. That's 35 miles north of Disney property, or about an hour by car in traffic.

Note that I don't recommend downtown Orlando, or, unless you're specifically looking for adult entertainment, the South Orange Blossom Trail (U.S. 441, known around town as the South Trail or SOBT).

My Short List

Worth-It Rating: 5

The following are my favorite hotels in Orlando, with the least expensive first.

RODEWAY INTERNATIONAL INN This clean, travel-class motel usually posts the area's lowest rates. The restaurant serves buffet-style, and there's a Japanese steakhouse. *6327 International Dr., Orlando 32819, tel. 407/351–4444 or 800/999–6327. 315 rooms. 2 restaurants, bar, VCRs, baby-sitting, supervised children's program (summer only). Pets accepted.*
$

DISNEY'S ALL-STAR RESORTS These are the best of the moderately priced properties at Walt Disney World. It's hard

to beat the price, anywhere. The **All-Star Sports Resort** can be recognized by its giant football helmet, immense basketball, and other sports artifacts—all oversized. The **All-Star Music Resort** features giant guitar, huge piano, and jumbo juke box. Their pools (there are four) are like mini–water parks on the same themes. Staying at either gets you all Disney privileges, including unlimited free Disney transportation. It almost doesn't matter that the rooms are a little small. *3,840 rooms. 2 restaurants, 2 bars, baby-sitting.*
$$

HOLIDAY INN MAINGATE EAST I rate this property one of the best on U.S. 192 in its price range. Even among Orlando hotels, most of which are family-friendly, this one stands out. Free child care runs from 8 AM until midnight, and kids eat free with their parents. You can't get any better than that. There are two swimming pools. *5678 W. Irlo Bronson Memorial Hwy., Kissimmee 34746, tel. 407/396–4488 or 800/FON–KIDS. 614 rooms, 89 suites. 2 restaurants, 2 bars, kitchenettes, VCRs, 2 hot tubs, lighted tennis court, health club, baby-sitting, supervised children's program, playground. Pets accepted.*
$$

TRAVELODGE HOTEL MAINGATE EAST This five-story highrise is my other pick on U.S. 192 in the moderate price range. It's very secure, since access to every room is by way of interior hallways. And it has all the facilities you need, plus free transportation to and from WDW attractions, at very competitive rates. *5711 W. Irlo Bronson Memorial Hwy., Kissimmee 34746, tel. 407/396–4222 or 800/327–1128. 444 rooms. Restaurant, 2 bars, kitchenettes, hot tub, baby-sitting.*
$$

DISNEY'S FORT WILDERNESS RESORT At my daughter Tiffany's request, we spent her fourth birthday at this campground and had a great time. It's complete with campfire sing-alongs (Chip and Dale show up), marshmallow roasts, and outdoor movies (some not screened anywhere else in the world). Don't let the campground idea keep you away if you're not a camper. There are tent sites and RV sites. But there are also spiffy free-standing Disney manufactured homes for rent (like deluxe RVs on foundations), with suite-size accommodations with full kitchens at rates you pay elsewhere on property for regular rooms. Plus, there are three swimming pools, loads of other facilities, unlimited free Disney transportation on property, and a location right next to River Country. *408 rooms, 387 RV sites, 390 tent sites. 2 restaurants, bar, kitchenettes, lake, lighted tennis court, horseback riding, boating, fishing, nature trails, baby-sitting, playground.*
$$–$$$

LANGFORD RESORT HOTEL If you want to get away from the crowds, this grand old resort in fashionable Winter Park is a good bet. Its buffet restaurant has an excellent Sunday brunch. *300 E. New England Ave., Winter Park 32789-4400, tel. 407/644–3400. 220 rooms, 11 themed suites. Restaurant, bar, kitchenettes. Pets accepted.*
$$–$$$

MARRIOTT'S ORLANDO WORLD CENTER This gorgeous, towering resort complex is the best hotel not only in the Lake Buena Vista area but in all Orlando. General Manager Jim McDonnell runs the tightest ship in town. You can't miss it, near Epcot's main entrance. It's the area's tallest structure, spectacularly panoramic. From higher floors, you can get the clearest aerial view of all three parks, anywhere. The free-form pool is amazing, with cascading waterfalls and a water slide,

and there are four others. *8701 World Center Dr., Orlando 32821, tel. 407/239–4200 or 800/228–9290. 1,503 rooms. 6 restaurants, 2 bars, 3 hot tubs, golf, miniature golf, 8 lighted tennis courts, health club, baby-sitting, supervised children's program, playground.*
$$$

STAR ISLAND/RESORT WORLD This is my pick as Central Florida's very best time-share resort—and you don't have to be a time-share owner to stay here. As home to Universal Studios Florida, Disney–MGM Studios, and many, many movie productions, TV shows, and sporting events, my home town regularly plays host to celebrities. Star Island was established to attract and accommodate them in style while remaining affordable to family vacationers. It was recently the site of a NFL Hall of Fame dinner, and every year it hosts the annual NBA Fantasy Basketball Camp.

All units are 1,400-square-foot suites with a wet bar, large-screen color TV, VCR, stereo system, and balcony in the living room; large TVs in every bedroom; and giant sunken whirlpool tubs in the master baths. Swimming, fishing, boating, lake cruises, water skiing, and jet skiing are all available on the lake. The playground is large and elaborate, complete with castle and pirate ship. There are four swimming pools, an elaborate health club, and a T.G.I. Friday's. On the shores of Lake Lucille, on U.S. 192 near Magic Kingdom's main gate and just down the street from Disney's Celebration, it's an unbelievable value. *2800 N. Poinciana Blvd., Kissimmee 34746-5258, tel. 407/397–7827 or 800/423–8604. 407 rooms. 3 restaurants, 2 bars, complimentary breakfast, kitchens, VCRs, lake, hot tubs, golf, miniature golf, 6 lighted tennis courts, health club, boating, baby-sitting, supervised children's program, playground.*
$$$

Other Good Bets

Worth-It Rating: 4

AT WDW

Remember that transportation to and from all the major attractions at WDW is free to guests at Disney-owned hotels.

DISNEY'S DIXIE LANDINGS RESORT Mark Twain's Tom Sawyer–Huck Finn world was a favorite recurrent theme of Walt Disney. This moderately priced Disney resort fits right in, conjuring up the look and feel of a riverboat landing. There are six swimming pools; the fanciest one has slides, swings, playgrounds, and a quiet area for anyone who insists on acting like a grown-up. *2,048 rooms. Restaurant, bar, lake, golf, boating, playground.*
$$

DISNEY'S PORT ORLEANS RESORT The sound system plays New Orleans jazz in this Disney version of a Bourbon Street bivouac. The pool, a mini–water park, has a Little Mermaid theme, and the slide is supposed to be King Neptune's. *1,008 rooms. Restaurant, lake, wading pool, hot tub, health club, boating, baby-sitting.*
$$

DISNEY'S BOARDWALK INN Our new favorite is a faithful re-creation of the Atlantic City I remember from the 50s. The New Jersey seaside architecture is perfectly detailed, right down to the giant Art Deco signs. And the fun never stops in the BoardWalk shopping, dining, and entertainment attraction at your doorstep. The Luna Park water play area features

a flume-like 200-foot slide. *378 rooms and suites. 4 restaurants, 4 bars, kitchenettes, lake, hot tub, golf, miniature golf, 2 lighted tennis courts, health club, boating, baby-sitting, supervised children's program, playground.*
$$$

DISNEY'S OLD KEY WEST RESORT This all-suite resort is part of the Disney Vacation Club time-share program. However, you don't have to buy one of the units to stay here, and they're perfectly appointed and extremely spacious. Like many romantics, my wife, Terrie, loves lighthouses. This place has several, including an impressive example that's the centerpiece of the dolphin-theme pool area, a mini–water park. This is actually one of four (count 'em) swimming pools. *497 suites. 2 restaurants, 2 bars, lake, 2 hot tubs, golf, 2 lighted tennis courts, health club, boating, baby-sitting, supervised children's program, playground, kitchens.*
$$$

DISNEY'S POLYNESIAN VILLAGE RESORT Imagine the huts of a Polynesian village, blown up to giant size. That's the Poly, as it's known informally around here. On the shores of the Seven Seas Lagoon, it's directly across the water from the Magic Kingdom, so guests get a clear view of the Magic Kingdom fireworks, and the floating Electrical Water Pageant makes its first nightly stop here at 9 PM. Of the several big-ticket resorts in the Magic Kingdom area, this is my top pick. The Contemporary (a bit dated), the newish Wilderness Lodge, and the Grand Floridian (extravagantly Victorian) can't hold a candle to the Poly for sheer charm and Disney lovability. The Poly is also the site of the Ohana Grill (and its fabulous island-theme show-and-feast), the wonderful Neverland Club (a kids' program), and WDW's beloved Polynesian Luau; though all three are open to all, they're most convenient to Poly guests. *853*

rooms, *12 suites. 3 restaurants, bar, lake, golf, health club, boating, baby-sitting, supervised children's program, playground.*
$$$

DISNEY'S VILLAS These villas come in several styles. The Treehouses, surrounded by woods, are a personal favorite—two-story houses with a spiral staircase between floors and one bedroom downstairs and two, with balconies, upstairs. The two-story townhouses are similar in size, though more traditional. And there are five swimming pools! *585 suites. Restaurant, bar, kitchenettes, lake, hot tub, golf, lighted tennis courts, health club, boating, baby-sitting, playground.*
$$$

DISNEY'S WILDERNESS LODGE Not many Florida hotels have fireplaces. But at this upscale re-creation of a Rocky Mountain resort, they're part of the theme. So are the waterfalls and the slide down huge rocks at the mini–water park/pool. There's also another pool that's more basic. *699 rooms, 29 suites. 2 restaurants, bar, lake, golf, boating, baby-sitting, supervised children's program. Pets accepted.*
$$$

DISNEY'S YACHT AND BEACH CLUB RESORT These lakeside siblings are almost like a single hotel, sharing amenities such as a mini–water park complete with a shipwreck where your pint-sized swabs can climb up to a crow's nest, then take a wet slide down the plank and a plunk into the not-at-all-briny deep. Both hotels look as if they were moved straight from some vintage northeastern seaside resort. *1,219 rooms, 71 concierge rooms, 40 suites. 2 restaurants, 4 bars, lake, golf, 2 lighted tennis courts, health club, boating, video games, baby-sitting, supervised children's program, playground.*
$$$

OTHER GOOD BETS

DOUBLETREE GUEST SUITES If your family has five or more and you want to spread out, this place is a very good deal. The price is right (not too much more than Disney's own bottom-of-the-line properties, which sleep just four to a room), and every unit is a suite, including a living room with a double sleep sofa and either one bedrooms (sleeping six) or two bedrooms (sleeping ten), each bedroom with two double beds or a king and a TV. *2305 Hotel Plaza Blvd., Lake Buena Vista 32830, tel. 407/934–1000. 229 units. Restaurant, bar, hot tub, lighted tennis court.*
$$$

LAKE BUENA VISTA

COMFORT INN LAKE BUENA VISTA This very clean, well-maintained complex has four buildings, each five stories, plus two swimming pools. You can see it from I–4 and it's convenient to Downtown Disney, with free transportation to and from WDW. Kids eat free. *8442 Palm Pkwy., Orlando 32836, tel. 407/239–7300 or 800/999–7300. 640 rooms. Restaurant, bar. Pets accepted.*
$–$$

DAYS INN LAKE BUENA VISTA RESORT I have found Days Inns to be inconsistent, this is one of the better ones. It's surprisingly well-decorated, rooms are oversized, and kids 12 and under eat free. Transportation to and from WDW attractions is free. *12205 Apopka-Vineland Rd., Orlando 32836, tel. 407/239–0444 or 800/423–3297. 390 rooms, 94 junior suites. 2 restaurants, bar, kitchenettes, playground.*
$$

DAYS INN LAKE BUENA VISTA VILLAGE One of the area's best Days Inns is the newly renovated seven-story property next to Walt Disney World Village. There's a microwave and coffeemaker on each floor, kids eat free, and transportation to and from WDW theme parks is free. *12490 Apopka-Vineland Rd., Orlando 32836, tel. 407/239–4646 or 800/521–3297. 245 rooms. Restaurant, bar, hot tub, baby-sitting. Pets accepted.* **$$**

INTERNATIONAL DRIVE

HOWARD JOHNSON This three-story motel has clean rooms at comfortable rates. It's equally convenient to Universal, Wet 'n' Wild, and Sea World. *6603 International Dr., Orlando 32819, tel. 407/351–2900 or 800/722–2900. 174 rooms. Restaurant (breakfast only), health club. Pets accepted.* **$**

QUALITY INN INTERNATIONAL Proof that all motels are not created equal, this Quality Inn has gated entrances, clean, spacious rooms, two swimming pools, and some of the consistently lowest rates on the strip. Kids eat free at the restaurant, which serves all-you-can-eat buffets at breakfast and dinner. Next door is Mickey D's, the world's largest McDonald's. *7600 International Dr., Orlando 32819, tel. 407/351–1600 or 800/875–7600. 728 rooms. Restaurant, bar. Pets accepted.* **$**

TRAVELODGE ORLANDO FLAGS This typical roadside motel with outdoor access is usually very inexpensive (plus, there's free transportation to and from major attractions). And it's almost as close to Universal Studios as you can get. *5858 Inter-*

national Dr., Orlando 32819, tel. 407/351–4410 or 800/722–7462. 269 rooms. Restaurant, bar, complimentary breakfast, hot tub, playground.
$

DAYS INN LAKESIDE There are three pools plus a lakefront beach with boating and picnicking at this motel just a couple of blocks off I-Drive. *7335 Sand Lake Rd., Orlando 32819, tel. 407/351–1900 or 800/777–3297. 693 rooms, 60 efficiencies, 24 suites. Restaurant, bar, lake, baby-sitting, 3 playgrounds.*
$$

DELTA ORLANDO RESORT This 25-acre resort is near the entrance to Universal Studios, and provides free transportation there and to Sea World and Wet 'n' Wild. Grounds are large and spacious, with well-planned and well-maintained recreational areas, including three swimming pools and two wading pools. *5715 Major Blvd., Orlando 32819-7988, tel. 407/351–3340. 800 rooms. 3 restaurants, bar, 3 hot tubs, miniature golf, 2 lighted tennis courts, supervised children's program, playground. Pets accepted.*
$$

FLORIDIAN OF ORLANDO You will almost always find one of the lowest rates on the strip at this hotel right next to Wet 'n' Wild. Suites have microwaves. *7299 Republic Dr., Orlando 32819, tel. 407/351–5009 or 800/445–7299. 304 rooms, 12 suites. Restaurant, bar, VCRs, lighted tennis court. Pets accepted.*
$$

HOLIDAY INN EXPRESS Holiday Inn Express is Holiday Inn's new chain of no-frills motels. However, this one opposite Wet 'n' Wild has most of the regular amenities, plus free transportation to and from WDW. *6323 International Dr.,*

Orlando 32819, tel. 407/351–4430 or 800/365–6935. 217 rooms. Complimentary breakfast.
$$

HOWARD JOHNSON UNIVERSAL TOWER This 20-story cylinder, visible from both I–4 and most of I-Drive, is one of the area's best-known landmarks. You're only a few blocks from Universal on one side and Wet 'n' Wild on the other (free rides are available to both and to Sea World). Rooms and suites on the top floor have some of the best views in town. *5905 International Dr., Orlando 32819, tel. 407/351–2100 or 800/327–1366. 302 rooms. 2 restaurants, bar, VCRs, hot tub, baby-sitting.*
$$

TWIN TOWERS HOTEL & CONVENTION CENTER You can't get any closer to Universal Studios. The illuminated towers make this is a major landmark of the Universal Studios area. The hotel's proximity to the studio makes it a frequent choice of visiting celebrities. *5780 Major Blvd., Orlando 32819, tel. 407/351–1000 or 800/843–8693. 760 rooms, 27 suites. Restaurant, 3 bars, hot tub, health club, baby-sitting, playground.*
$$

CLARION PLAZA HOTEL This 12-story hotel near the convention center gives lots of facilities for the money. *9700 International Dr., Orlando 32819-8114, tel. 407/352–9700 or 800/627–8258. 810 rooms, 32 suites. 2 restaurants, bars, VCRs, golf, baby-sitting, playground.*
$$$

HOLIDAY INN INTERNATIONAL DRIVE RESORT At this 13-acre tropical resort, service is great and the facilities well above par. *6515 International Dr., Orlando 32819, tel. 407/351–*

3500 or 800/465–4329. 652 rooms. 2 restaurants, bar, health club, baby-sitting.
$$$

PEABODY HOTEL ORLANDO This 27-story hotel is famous as home of the Peabody ducks. Every day, in an amazing daily spectacle, they take the elevator to the ground floor, and then, to the strains of John Phillip Sousa, march through the lobby to the fountain in the middle. Every afternoon the ceremony is reversed. The restaurants are among Orlando's best. *9801 International Dr., Orlando 32819, tel. 407/352–4000 or 800/PEABODY. 891 rooms, 57 suites. 3 restaurants, 2 bars, hot tub, 4 lighted tennis courts, health club, baby-sitting.*
$$$

U.S. 192/KISSIMMEE

RAMADA LIMITED This nice, clean motel across from Wild Bill's and Fort Liberty usually posts very low rates. And there are video games in the rooms. *5055 W. Irlo Bronson Memorial Hwy., Kissimmee 34746, tel. 407/396–2212 or 800/446–5669. 107 rooms. Complimentary breakfast. Pets accepted.*
$

DAYS INN/SUITES EAST OF MAGIC KINGDOM Kids eat free and you can buy up to 10 gallons of gas half-price at this motel next to the Old Town shopping-dining-rides attraction. *5820 W. Irlo Bronson Memorial Hwy., Kissimmee 34746, tel. 407/396–7900 or 800/327–9126. 404 rooms, 604 suites. 4 restaurants, complimentary breakfast, kitchenettes, hot tub, health club, baby-sitting, playground. Pets accepted.*
$–$$

BEST WESTERN MAINGATE Transportation to and from WDW is free at this clean, well-located property. *8600 W. Irlo Bronson Hwy., Kissimmee 34747, tel. 407/396–0100 or 800/ 528–1234. 300 rooms. Restaurant, bar, coffeemakers.*
$$

HOLIDAY INN KISSIMMEE DOWNTOWN Newly renovated, this hotel is now one of the nicest on the U.S. 192 strip, with lush landscaping, two pools, a bright lobby, and refurbished rooms. The Black Angus Steakhouse, on premises, is a favorite among locals and one of the area's better eateries. *2009 W. Vine St., Kissimmee 34741, tel. 407/846–2713. 200 rooms. Restaurant, bar, kitchenettes, hot tub, lighted tennis court, playground. Pets accepted.*
$$

HOLIDAY INN NIKKI BIRD RESORT Rooms are beautifully decorated here. There are three swimming pools and two wading pools. Kids eat free, and rides to WDW are on the house. Home of Angel's Lobster Feast. *7300 W. Bronson Hwy., Kissimmee 34746, tel. 407/396–7300 or 800/206–2747. 529 rooms. Restaurant, bar, 3 hot tubs, lighted tennis court, playground.*
$$

HYATT ORLANDO Dominating the corner of I–4 and U.S. 192, this rambling, well-appointed 56-acre resort with four swimming pools and a wading pool at each is one of the most convenient in the area. It's not your usual Hyatt—actually, it's a lot more like a Holiday Inn. It doesn't charge typical Hyatt rates either. *6375 W. Irlo Bronson Memorial Hwy., Kissimmee 34746, tel. 407/396–1234 or 800/233–1234. 922 rooms, 29 suites. 4 restaurants, bar, 4 hot tubs, 3 lighted tennis courts, health club, baby-sitting, playground.*
$$

OTHER GOOD BETS

TRAVELODGE SUITES EAST GATE In this attractive budget property near S.R. 535, rates for suites are some of the lowest on the strip. And all units are suites. *5399 W. Irlo Bronson Memorial Hwy., Kissimmee 34746, tel. 407/396–7666 or 800/ 457–8483. 157 suites. Kitchenettes, wading pool, hot tub, playground. Pets accepted.*
$$

chapter 15

AFTER DARK

Church Street, Pleasure Island, Disney's BoardWalk

When promoter Bob Snow came to Orlando back in the early 1970s, he wanted to revitalize its shabby downtown by turning it into a dining and shopping attraction with a historic flavor. Although problems had dogged his efforts to do the same thing in Pensacola, he was wildly successful in Orlando. For years, until Disney created Pleasure Island, his Church Street Station was synonymous with Orlando nightlife in the minds of tourists.

CHURCH STREET STATION It started out as a complex of restaurants and night spots occupying local landmarks like Orlando pioneer Stanley Bumby's hundred-year-old hardware store, a place I often visited as a child. Bob Snow and his successors scoured the world and filled the complex with 19th-century metal ceiling tiles, hand-carved woodwork, church pews, chandeliers, and stained glass. Vintage flying machines from hot-air balloons to biplanes are suspended from the ceilings, and the stuffed game animal heads adorn the walls. Rare and expensive antique vehicles are parked in the street, including a highly prized 1939 Duesenberg; a 1912 steam engine and old Pullman cars are stopped on the old train tracks. It's an eclectic visual tour de force.

Admission is free to nearby dining-and-shopping complexes, adjacent Church Street Exchange and to Church Street Market, across the street. But after 6 PM, you have to pay a cover charge to enter Church Street Station, and food and beverages are extra and pricey. You're expected to buy a drink or two, at around $4 a pop, in each of its night spots. So for a couple, it's easy to go through a couple of hundred dollars in an evening.

If you're prepared to spend the bucks, be prepared for a good time. Church Street Station is a loud, rowdy, in-your-face place to party hearty. There are four nightclubs, three with scheduled sets; showtimes are staggered so that you can take in a set in each during an evening. **Rosie O'Grady's** is a New Orleans–style jazz club where you can snack on a burger to the strains of an enthusiastic Dixieland band. Waiters and waitresses even dance on the bar. The **Orchid Garden Ballroom**, done up in Victorian style with rich woods and decorative glass, has a high-powered 50s-style rock band for dancing. And many major country stars have performed in the **Cheyenne Saloon and Opera House,** a Western music hall featured on numerous national TV shows. Intricate carved woodwork encloses several levels of balconies, and you can order Wild West fare—buffalo, beef steaks, chicken, and ribs (entrées $12.50 and up).

Phineas Phogg's Balloon Works, the fourth club, is a non-stop modern dance and rock club, mostly for Gen X-ers. It's full of vintage balloonist's paraphernalia. There are also a couple of restaurants. In turn-of-the-century-style **Lili Mar-**

lene's **Aviator's Pub and Restaurant,** the prime rib comes in generous portions au jus or blackened. Entrées are about $20. The very casual **Crackers Oyster Bar,** which reminds me of the old fish camps that still dot Florida, does a more than respectable job with fresh Florida seafood, and serves everything from raw oysters to a nice lobster-and-clam bake. The specialty is a tangy Pensacola clam chowder, but I like the chef's chili—loaded with gator meat. This place doubles as a sports bar. Entrées cost between $9.95 and $25.

Lunchtime, when Church Street Station levies no cover, is great for soaking up the atmosphere without paying. There's also an excellent Sunday brunch buffet at Lili Marlene's ($10.95) and an all-you-can-eat Friday barbecue lunch at the Cheyenne saloon ($7.95). And tours of the complex are available. The area is also home to several other excellent clubs and restaurants.

The Fast Track: Shows are timed so that you can catch them all in an evening by going from one to the next. So that's what everybody does. Before you start out, pop your head into each of the three music spots to see which is least crowded, and start there. Then you'll be moving from venue to venue with the smallest group. *129 W. Church St., 407/422–2434 (ext. 427, to find out about tours of the complex). Cover $16.95 adults, $10.95 children 4–12. Church Street night spots open daily 11 AM–2 AM, shops open 11–11.*

Worth-It Rating: 3+

PLEASURE ISLAND Though Church Street Station and Pleasure Island are based on an identical concept, there is an attitude difference between the two that is generational. Though Bob Snow has been gone from CSS for several years, his stamp on it is indelible and it is a place designed by and for the World War II generation. Pleasure Island caters more to Baby Boomers and Gen X-ers. If you're going to just one nightlife attraction, there's no contest in my mind: Pleasure Island has much more than Church Street.

At the **Comedy Warehouse,** comics of national caliber do stand-up and improv. Hipsters dig live sounds ranging from swing to fusion at the **Pleasure Island Jazz Company. Mannequin's Dance Palace** features contemporary music and a dazzling light show. And you can wear your hip-huggers to 8Trax, the 70s disco palace with pulsing lights underneath a translucent dance floor. The **Rock & Roll Beach Club** is three stories of oldies, often with name talent. The **Neon Armadillo Music Saloon** also books country-and-western talent. The **Adventurers Club** defies simple description. In one spooky room, primitive masks suddenly start to talk; in the salon, adventurers regale guests with tall tales. Outside, there's more live entertainment on the **West End Stage.** Every night at midnight, the folks at Pleasure Island remind you that tomorrow is the first day of the rest of your life with a New Year's celebration, complete with fireworks. Once you've bought the pay-one-price general admission ticket, you can enter any of these clubs for free.

Without paying the general admission, you can take your pick of flicks at the adjacent 24-screen AMC movie complex, you can shop in the shops, and you can eat in the restaurants. The **Fireworks Factory** has an eclectic American menu but lots of barbecue (I love the crab cakes—they're even better than the huge shrimp); entrées range from $13.95 to $15. The **Portobello Yacht Club** next door is an excellent Northern Italian seafood restaurant with reasonable prices—several entrées are under $20. **Fulton's Crab House,** which also serves seafood, has taken over the old Empress Lilly paddle wheeler. Restaurants, shops, and movie theater are open during the day as well as at night. *Walt Disney World Village, tel. 407/934–7781. Cover $17.95. Clubs open daily 7 PM–2 AM, shops 11 AM–2 AM.* **Worth-It Rating: 5**

DISNEY BOARDWALK My wife, Terrie, and I fell in love with this place at first sight. Designed in classic New England style to re-create the old boardwalks built along the northeastern beaches just after the turn of the century, this area has shopping, dining, lodging, and entertainment. Admission to the whole complex is free, and—here's the best part—there are no cover charges at any of the clubs! (The **BoardWalk Inn** and the **BoardWalk Villas** are both part of the Disney Vacation Club's time-share operation, but you don't have to be a time-share owner to stay there or party at their bars and clubs.) The boardwalk overlooks a lagoon facing the Yacht and Beach Club, their lighthouse, and the pirate ship at their mini–water park. Epcot is to your right, and you can see the Eiffel Tower in the distance, rising just above the Board-Walk's gazebo. The promenade is wide enough to allow crowds to peacefully coexist with the 10-passenger canopied bicycles called Surrey Bikes, available for rent at $3 an hour or $10 a day between 10 and 6 and sometimes at night as well. Away from the water are a handful of shops and an arcade with pinball and video games (I hate arcades—Ricky, my son, hits the arcade and bang, that's the end of 20 bucks and we haven't even done anything).

What keeps us coming back to the BoardWalk are the clubs. The **Atlantic Dance Club** recalls the ballrooms that broadcast swing music in the 1940s. The **ESPN Club** is the ultimate sports bar, with monitors everywhere—all tuned to ESPN, of course. **Jellyroll's** is a big, rollicking night spot with two piano players at dueling grand pianos. It's the kind of place where you'd expect a cover, but there is none. (In fact, Blazing Pianos at the Mercado, which I describe in Chapters 12 and 13, offers the same concept but with a $10 cover.) In the **Belle Vue Room**, a lakeside lounge, the elegant decor and formally attired waiters make you feel like the Great Gatsby. **Big River Grill and Brewing Works** is Disney's own microbrewery; it serves British pub fare like sausages and meat pies. At **BoardWalk Bakery,** bakers bake a lot of bread right before your eyes, along with pastries and sweets. The **Flying Fish Café** serves fresh seafood, with entrées from $15 to $24. A house specialty is scallops with black truffle risotto. Reservations are accepted. Besides its highly entertaining show of pizza-twirling, **Spoodles** has a Mediterranean menu that includes some very good grilled lamb chops and a Moroccan vegetable platter, among other fairly exotic dishes. (Reservations are a good idea.) The bars in the BoardWalk Inn and BoardWalk Villas are every bit as atmospheric and fun. Terrie and I love all the old Atlantic City pictures displayed in these hotels—wonderful bits of nostalgia that date back to what the kids have dubbed the "gray-and-white days." There's even a picture of Atlantic City's famous diving horse.

And what would a boardwalk be without taffy? Hit **Seashore Sweets.** On our last visit, a boardwalk magician delighted the children with a show during which he was able to extract a variety of exotic objects from their ears. All in all, the BoardWalk is charming, nostalgic, and entertaining—as well as being the home of some of the best deals on Disney property. *2101 N. Epcot Resort Blvd., Lake Buena Vista, tel. 407/939–3420; 407/560–8754 to reserve Surrey Bikes or get information on their availability; and 407/WDW–DINE for restaurant reservations. Clubs open daily 7 PM–2 AM, shops open daily 9 AM–1 AM.*

Worth-It Rating: 5

chapter 16

BEACH, BEACH, BEACH

Florida's Atlantic Beaches

F lorida's East Coast is closer to Orlando than the Gulf of Mexico, about an hour by car. Each beach town has a unique flavor. Driving is permitted on the sand in some—catching some rays alongside an active roadway can take some getting used to, so choose your beach accordingly.

DAYTONA BEACH AND NORTH

DAYTONA BEACH Back at the turn of the century, people raced their cars on the hard-packed white sand at Daytona, about an hour from Orlando and one of the easiest beaches to reach. Since then, driving on the beach has been a distinguishing feature of Daytona life. Traffic is kept to a crawl and restricted to designated lanes. Still, it can be risky—occasionally, an errant car does run over a pedestrian or two.

On the other hand, along with the cars you'll find motorized snack carts, which offer munchables, sodas, even sand castle–building aids, and rent beach umbrellas, boogieboards, and motor scooters. The surf is moderate, with prime East Coast waves for surfing and body-surfing. Surf-fishing is allowed early in the morning and away from bathers.

More college students flock to Daytona than anywhere else in the world during spring break. So between February and May, you may have trouble finding a room, and when you do, you may find yourself sandwiched between rowdy drinking parties. The spring break reputation has made Daytona the place to see hard bodies in skimpy bathing suits the rest of the year, too. Which is why the producers of *Baywatch* have begun production on a new series, *Daytona.*

The **Daytona International Speedway** (1801 W. International Speedway, tel. 904/254–2700) is another major player in town. Its biggest annual events are **Bike Week,** a celebration of motorcycle racing in early March, and the **Daytona 500** auto race in February. Its new **Daytona USA** is a must-see only for serious enthusiasts.

Because the Speedway dominates local politics, Daytona has rolled out the red carpet for America's motorcycle gangs. Establishments offering adult entertainment, tattooing, and body-piercing have become ubiquitous, making some families uncomfortable.

Information: Convention & Visitors Bureau, 126 E. Orange Ave., Daytona Beach, 32114-4406, tel. 904/255–0415. Destination Daytona, 1801 Volusia Ave., Daytona Beach 32114, tel. 904/253–8669.

Worth-It Rating: 2. Add 1 if you're a race fan.

ORMOND BEACH Immediately north and adjacent to Daytona, Ormond is Daytona without many of the problems—at least for the moment. While Ormond has its Ma and Pa motels, like the rest of the East Coast, most properties here are more upscale. Ormond is usually quieter and easier to get around in than its neighbor—except during spring break, race weeks, and Bike Week. During those times, Daytona has no city limits.

Information: Chamber of Commerce, 165 W. Granada Blvd., Ormond Beach, 32174-6303, tel. 904/677–3454.
Worth-It Rating: 4

ST. AUGUSTINE An hour north of Daytona is America's oldest city and one of Florida's best family destinations—mellow, educational, inexpensive, and lots of fun. The St. Augustine slogan says it all: "Eight miles of beach and the rest is history." The history begins with St. Augustine's discovery by Juan Ponce de León in 1513. Founded by Pedro Menendez de Aviles in 1565 on the shores of Mantanzas Bay, St. Augustine is the oldest continuously incorporated community in America—and it's loaded with things to see.

My favorite St. Augustine destination is **O.C. White's restaurant** (118 Av. Menendez), in an 18th-century onetime pirate residence. Owner David White regales diners with tales of the home's notorious past and of its current ghostly residents (featured on TV's *Sightings*). *The Cross and Sword* (1 Riberia St.), the Florida state play, is a spectacular dramatization of the early struggles for control of the area, performed in an amphitheater carved out of the palmetto-scrub jungle. Bring mosquito repellent.

St. Augustine's best beach is on beautiful **Anastasia Island.** You can drive on some stretches of it, but the best parts are accessible only on foot or from beachfront hotels. The surf is moderate and the beach composed of rare coquina—tiny, pulverized shells mixed with dark sand. Old hotels and vintage bed-and-breakfasts abound, along with chain motels.

Information: Visitor Information Center, 1 Riberia St., St. Augustine, 32084, tel. 904/825–1000.
Worth-It Rating: 5+

SOUTH OF DAYTONA

NEW SMYRNA BEACH The site of the Namey family condo is immediately south of Daytona, a quiet, secluded family beach. It stays that way, too, because there are no major four-lane roads into the area from Orlando. Hotels are few and small. Instead, most people stay in individual condos or rentals such as the legendary **Roberto delMar** (3619 Hill St., New Smyrna Beach 32169, tel. 407/644–3292). To the south is the northern end of the **Canaveral National Seashore** (tel. 407/867–2805), part of the buffer zone around the Space Center and the site of the last totally unspoiled Florida beach. Here, we have petted manatees, watched dolphins frolic, and picked giant conch right off the sandy shore. I sincerely hope I'm not making the area sound too appealing. We would just as soon keep this off-the-path secret to ourselves.

Information: Chamber of Commerce, 115 Canal St., New Smyrna Beach, 32168-7003, tel. 904/428–2449. New Smyrna Beach Rentals, 4155 S. Atlantic Ave., #509, New Smyrna Beach, 32169-3793, tel. 800/609–7874.
Worth-It Rating: 5

COCOA AND THE SPACE COAST This is probably your best value on the East Coast. Easily accessible by the Bee-Line Expressway or on S.R. 50 east of Orlando, the beaches of Brevard County, known as the Space Coast, are family-friendly, safe, and reasonably priced. Many are part of the southern end of the Canaveral National Seashore (*see* Chapter 7).

Although the surf is moderate, Florida's biggest surfing waves are nearby, at the **Canaveral jetties** north of Cocoa Beach. Brevard beaches have soft, white sand, with occasional patches of coquina. Driving is not allowed, but there are beach concessions and oceanfront restaurants. Be aware that a state law makes it mandatory for all such establishments to continuously play Jimmy Buffett's "Margueritaville." If you find a beach bar that is not, you are required to immediately report it to local authorities.

The centerpiece of Cocoa Beach is **Ron Jon's Surf Shop** (4151 N. Atlantic Ave., Cocoa Beach, tel. 407/799–8820), the largest surf shop in the world, with more outdoor advertising than even Universal Studios Florida. Check it out.

Down the street is a favorite family eating spot, **Yen-Yen** Chinese restaurant (2 N. Atlantic Ave., Cocoa Beach, tel. 407/783–9512). This is not your typical chop suey joint; it serves Hong Kong–style cuisine. And we often travel to Titusville to stand in line at the popular **Dixie Crossroads** (1475 Garden St., Titusville, tel. 407/268–5000), which features all the Florida rock shrimp you can eat—they're split, broiled, and served hot, like tiny lobsters. It's not uncommon to spy an astronaut here.

At the north end of the Space Coast, north of Cocoa, is **Playalinda Beach.** It is part of the Canaveral National Seashore, although it is not connected by land to the section south of New Smyrna Beach. Playalinda often has nude or topless bathing, though its status changes with the complexion of local politics.

Information: Chamber of Commerce, 400 Fortenberry Rd., Merritt Island 32952, tel. 407/459–2200; Welcome Center, 1325 N. Atlantic Ave., Cocoa Beach, 32931-3220, tel. 407/783–8811; Chamber of Commerce, 1005 E. Strawbridge Ave., Melbourne, 32901-4740, tel. 407/724–5400.

Worth-It Rating: 4

SOUTH OF DAYTONA

index

coupons

coupons

coupons

DISNEY LIKE A PRO DISNEY LIKE A PRO DISNEY LIKE A PRO

coupons

coupons

Save $10.00
for
**One Hour
Massage Therapy
With this coupon**
only **$45.00**

Medi & Clinic   (407) 396-1195
House & Med

FREE
HEALTH
SCREENING

a $60.00 Value

Orlando Regional
Sand Lake Hospital
(407) 351-8506

coupons

coupons

DISNEY LIKE A PRO DISNEY LIKE A PRO DISNEY LIKE A PRO
DISNEY LIKE A PRO DISNEY LIKE A PRO DISNEY LIKE A PRO
DISNEY LIKE A PRO DISNEY LIKE A PRO DISNEY LIKE A PRO
DISNEY LIKE A PRO DISNEY LIKE A PRO DISNEY LIKE A PRO
DISNEY LIKE A PRO DISNEY LIKE A PRO DISNEY LIKE A PRO
DISNEY LIKE A PRO DISNEY LIKE A PRO DISNEY LIKE A PRO
DISNEY LIKE A PRO DISNEY LIKE A PRO DISNEY LIKE A PRO
DISNEY LIKE A PRO DISNEY LIKE A PRO DISNEY LIKE A PRO
DISNEY LIKE A PRO DISNEY LIKE A PRO DISNEY LIKE A PRO
DISNEY LIKE A PRO DISNEY LIKE A PRO DISNEY LIKE A PRO
DISNEY LIKE A PRO DISNEY LIKE A PRO DISNEY LIKE A PRO
DISNEY LIKE A PRO DISNEY LIKE A PRO DISNEY LIKE A PRO
DISNEY LIKE A PRO DISNEY LIKE A PRO DISNEY LIKE A PRO
DISNEY LIKE A PRO DISNEY LIKE A PRO DISNEY LIKE A PRO
DISNEY LIKE A PRO DISNEY LIKE A PRO DISNEY LIKE A PRO
DISNEY LIKE A PRO DISNEY LIKE A PRO DISNEY LIKE A PRO
DISNEY LIKE A PRO DISNEY LIKE A PRO DISNEY LIKE A PRO
DISNEY LIKE A PRO DISNEY LIKE A PRO DISNEY LIKE A PRO
DISNEY LIKE A PRO DISNEY LIKE A PRO DISNEY LIKE A PRO
DISNEY LIKE A PRO DISNEY LIKE A PRO DISNEY LIKE A PRO
DISNEY LIKE A PRO DISNEY LIKE A PRO DISNEY LIKE A PRO
DISNEY LIKE A PRO DISNEY LIKE A PRO DISNEY LIKE A PRO
DISNEY LIKE A PRO DISNEY LIKE A PRO DISNEY LIKE A PRO
DISNEY LIKE A PRO DISNEY LIKE A PRO DISNEY LIKE A PRO
DISNEY LIKE A PRO DISNEY LIKE A PRO DISNEY LIKE A PRO
DISNEY LIKE A PRO DISNEY LIKE A PRO DISNEY LIKE A PRO
DISNEY LIKE A PRO DISNEY LIKE A PRO DISNEY LIKE A PRO
DISNEY LIKE A PRO DISNEY LIKE A PRO DISNEY LIKE A PRO
DISNEY LIKE A PRO DISNEY LIKE A PRO DISNEY LIKE A PRO
DISNEY LIKE A PRO DISNEY LIKE A PRO DISNEY LIKE A PRO
DISNEY LIKE A PRO DISNEY LIKE A PRO DISNEY LIKE A PRO
DISNEY LIKE A PRO DISNEY LIKE A PRO DISNEY LIKE A PRO
DISNEY LIKE A PRO DISNEY LIKE A PRO DISNEY LIKE A PRO
DISNEY LIKE A PRO DISNEY LIKE A PRO DISNEY LIKE A PRO
DISNEY LIKE A PRO DISNEY LIKE A PRO DISNEY LIKE A PRO
DISNEY LIKE A PRO DISNEY LIKE A PRO DISNEY LIKE A PRO
DISNEY LIKE A PRO DISNEY LIKE A PRO DISNEY LIKE A PRO

coupons

coupons

Wet'n Wild.
INTERNATIONAL DRIVE, ORLANDO

$2 OFF
All Day Admission

Experience Wet 'N Wilds thrills for
$2 off the regular all day admission.
Coupon good for up to six people
not to be used in conjunction
with any other discounted offer
or afternoon pricing.

Fodor's
PLU6A
7C
DLAP

DOWNLOAD
OUR LATEST
COUPONS
ON YOUR
COMPUTER!

http://www.wdw4adults.com/coupons

attraction coupons

GATORLAND

Located at Hwy. 44 in S. Orlando
(407) 855-5496

10% OFF

Up to six people.
Not valid with any other offer.

CODE 189
DLAP

CHURCH STREET STATION

129 W. CHURCH STREET

$3.00 OFF

Up to $18.00 value up to six people.
Not appliable for special appearences or with any
other discounts. Not Valid on New Years Eve.
Adult Code 5636   Child Code 5637
Exp. 12/30/97
DLAP

FUN 'n WHEELS

6739 Sand Lake Rd. • Orlando • (407) 351-5651
3711 W. Vine St. • Kissimmee • (407) 870-2222

20 FREE Ride Tickets

with the purchase of 20 tickets
with this coupon.
DLAP

TOHO AIRBOAT EXCURSIONS

SEE MAP FOR LOCATION OR CALL
(407) 931-2225

$3.00 OFF EACH ADULT

Regular admission, adult price. No limit!
Also, kids under 7 are 1/2 price!
ON DAY TRIPS ONLY.
Not valid w/other discounts or coupons.
DLAP

CAPONE'S
DINNER & SHOW
(800) 220-8428

BUY 1 & GET 1 FREE!

Purchase adult ticket at regular price plus
tax, gratuity, and $6.49 ticketing charge,
not valid with other offers.
DLAP

WILD BILL'S

(800) 883-8181
5260 U.S. 192 • Kissimmee

UP TO $24 OFF

Present this coupon at check-in to receive $4 off
each adult admission and $2 off child admission.
Up to 6 people. Not valid with any other offer.
DLAP

KING HENRY'S FEAST

8984 International Dr. • 351-5151

UP TO $24 OFF

Present this coupon at check-in to receive $4 off
each adult admission and $2 off child admission.
Up to 6 people. Not valid with any other offer.
Tickets must be purchased at the King Henry's
Feast box office.
DLAP

FLYING TIGERS

231 N. Hoagland Blvd., Kissimmee

(407) 933-1942

50¢ OFF

each admission. Limit 6 with coupon.
DLAP

dining coupons

SHOGUN
AUTHENTIC JAPANESE STEAK HOUSE
6327 International Drive
IN THE RODEWAY INN INTERNATIONAL
352-1607

50% OFF

Buy One Entree, Get 2nd Entree of equal or
lesser value 1/2 price. Not valid with any other
offer. Please present to server when ordering.
DLAP

Dairy Queen®

6321 A. International Dr., Orlando

Dairy Queen® Sundae
50¢ OFF

Not valid with other offer.
DLAP

Captain Nemos
Seafood & Steak Resturant
5469 W. Hwy. 192 • Kissimmee, FL
(407) 396-6911

$2⁹⁹

BREAKFAST SPECIAL INCLUDES:
2 EGGS, 2 BACON, OR SAUSAGE
TOAST & JELLY, HOMEFRIES OR GRITS
Not valid with any other discounts or specials,
DLAP

Austin's
8633 International Dr., Orlando
(407) 363-9575

10% OFF

Bring this coupon and get
10% off your entire bill.

Not valid with other discounts or
promotions or on holidays.
DLAP

Dairy Queen®

6321 A. International Dr., Orlando

Blizzard® or Breeze®
75¢ OFF

Not valid with any other offer.
DLAP

Kobe
DINNER SHOW
6 Course Dinner
Steak, Chicken & Shrimp
REG. $19.95, NOW $12.95

Lobster, Steak & Chicken
REG. $23.95, NOW $16.95
Must present coupon before ordering.
Not valid with other offers.
12/31/97 EXPIRES
DLAP

Austin's
8633 International Dr., Orlando
(407) 363-9575

10% OFF

Bring this coupon and get
10% off your entire bill.

Not valid with other discounts or
promotions or on holidays.
DLAP

Captain Nemos
Seafood & Steak Resturant
5469 W. Hwy. 192 • Kissimmee, FL
(407) 396-6911

10% OFF
YOUR ENTIRE MEAL

Not valid with other offers or coupons.
DLAP

dining coupons

Arabian Nights

Located on 192 just minutes from Disney
(407) 239-9223

$4.00 OFF
PER PERSON, REGULAR ADMISSION

Present this coupon at the Arabian Nights box office and save. Limit 6 admissions per coupon. Not valid with other discounts, promotions or special events.   DLAP

PONDEROSA
STEAKHOUSE
Call (407) 352-9343 for a location nearest you

50¢ OFF
per adult

OUR GIGANTIC BREAKFAST BUFFET
7AM–11:30AM

Not valid with other discounts.

DLAP

PONDEROSA
STEAKHOUSE
Call (407) 352-9343 for a location nearest you

10% OFF
LUNCH OR DINNER

Not valid with other discounts.

DLAP

Dairy Queen®

6321 A. International Dr., Orlando

Banana Split® or Peanut Buster® Parfait
75¢ OFF

Not valid with any other offer.
DLAP

Dairy Queen®

6321 A. International Dr., Orlando

Foot Long Superdog®
50¢ OFF

Not valid with any other offer.
DLAP

Dairy Queen®

6321 A. International Dr., Orlando

Blizzard® or Breeze®
75¢ OFF

Not valid with any other offer.
DLAP

Dairy Queen®

6321 A. International Dr., Orlando

Dairy Queen® Milkshake
50¢ OFF

Not valid with any other offer.
DLAP

PONDEROSA
STEAKHOUSE
Call (407) 352-9343 for a location nearest you

10% OFF
LUNCH OR DINNER

Not valid with other discounts.

DLAP

shopping coupons

CITRUS HOUSE

4724 W. Irlo Bronson Memorial Hwy.
Kissimmee, FL 34746 • (407) 396-4391

FREE 5 LB BAG OF CITRUS

with a purchase of $10.00 and this coupon.
Only at time of purchase.
Limit one per customer.
DLAP

SHELL WORLD

4727 W. Irlo Bronson Hwy. (Hwy. 192)
Kissimmee, FL 34746
396-9000

5684 International Dr.
Orlando, FL 34746
370-3344

FREE SEASHELL BRACELET, NECKLACE
OR GENUINE FLORIDA SAND DOLLAR
No purchase necessary. Please, one coupon per family.
DLAP

CD PLANET

6550 International Dr. • Suite 103
Orlando • (407) 352-5500

$2.00 OFF

Not valid with any other discount coupons.
Limit one coupon per purchase.
DLAP

CD PLANET

6550 International Dr. • Suite 103
Orlando • (407) 352-5500

$2.00 OFF

Not valid with any other discount coupons.
Limit one coupon per purchase.
DLAP

SPORTS DOMINATOR

10% OFF

WITH COUPON ONLY
NOT VALID WITH ANY OTHER
OFFERS OR DISCOUNTS
DLAP

BARGAIN WORLD

10% OFF

WITH COUPON ONLY
NOT VALID WITH ANY OTHER
OFFERS OR DISCOUNTS
DLAP

CITRUS HOUSE

4724 W. Irlo Bronson Memorial Hwy.
Kissimmee, FL 34746 • (407) 396-4391

FREE 5 LB BAG OF CITRUS

with a purchase of $10.00 and this coupon.
Only at time of purchase.
Limit one per customer.
DLAP

SHELL WORLD

4727 W. Irlo Bronson Hwy. (Hwy. 192)
Kissimmee, FL 34746
396-9000

5684 International Dr.
Orlando, FL 34746
370-3344

FREE SEASHELL BRACELET, NECKLACE
OR GENUINE FLORIDA SAND DOLLAR
No purchase necessary. Please, one coupon per family.
DLAP

DISNEY LIKE A PRO

coupons

DESTINATION UNIVERSAL
CELEBRITY VACATION PACKAGE™
Get the Red Carpet Treatment
from $169*

The Celebrity Vacation Package™ rolls out the red carpet for you in ways you can't imagine. You'll feel like a mega star as you enjoy all the exclusive benefits this fabulous vacation package offers.

Your Celebrity Vacation Package™ includes:
- 3 or more nights' hotel accommodations (including hotel taxes).
- A Vacation Value Pass**
  Featuring **Unlimited Admission** for up to three days to: Universal Studios Florida, Sea Word of Florida and Wet 'n Wild, Florida. **Plus extra 2 days FREE.**
- Your choice of one lunch or dinner meal feature at the following full service restaurants*** (per person): **Universal Studios Florida's Studio Stars, Finnegans Bar & Grill, Hard Rock Cafe**®
- **Unlimited Transportation** from your hotel to Universal Studios Florida, Sea World of Florida and Wet 'n Wild, Florida.
- **Early park admission** to Universal Studios Florida on select days.

Optional air-fare, Avis car rental or round-trip airport transfers available.

* Price based on land only package.
** Valid for 3 days only.
*** Includes tax and gratuity. Certain menu restrictions may apply. Package pricing restrictions may apply, package price good through 12/15/97.

FOR RESERVATIONS AND INFORMATION
CONTACT YOUR TRAVEL AGENT OR CALL

(800) 224-3838
ASK ABOUT OUR NEW 1997 PACKAGES
Presented by: The Universal City Travel Company™
DLAP

coupons

PIRATE'S DINNER ADVENTURE
Orlando, Florida

$5 OFF
reservations are recommended

6400 Carrier Drive, just off International Drive
(800) 866-2469   (407) 248-0590

Ahoy Matey! Presenting Orlando's Newest Treasure, an action packed musical that includes stunts and dazzling special effects. The dinning room features a full scale pirateship afloat in a 300 thousand gallon lagoon. There you will dine on a delicious three-course pirate feast, complete with cold frosty beverages. There is something for everyone at Pirates, Where Adventure Never Ends.

Adult admission ($33.95 plus tax), child admission ($19.95 plus tax).
Coupon is valid with any other discounts and is redeemable until 12/30/97.

DLAP

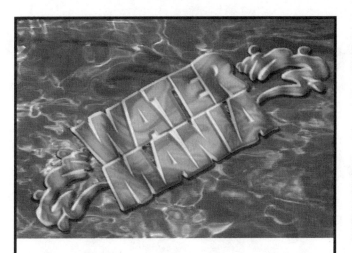

Florida's Family Water Park
Save up to $24

Enjoy 36 fun acres of stimulating slides,
adventurous flumes, numerous children's
playgrounds, large wave pool,
volleyball courts, and three acres of
beautifully landscaped picnic areas.

1/2 mile of I-4 on U.S.-192
11/2 miles east of Disney World
(407) 396-2626

Not valid with any other discounts. Good for up to 6 people.
CODE 708/7079
DLAP

SAVE OVER $1,000
IN ORLANDO
J U S T L I K E M A G I C

Get the card that lets you save over $1000 on
attractions, accommodations, dining, transportation
and shopping in Orlando.

For your free Magicard™, call (800) 643-0482,
contact us at our internet address,
http://www.goflorida.com/orlando,
or stop by our Official Visitor Information Center.

DLAP

DISNEY LIKE A PRO

ADMISSION PRICES AND INFORMATION

If you're visiting Universal Studios, Sea World, and Wet 'n Wild, don't forget about the five-day multipark **Value Pass** ($89.95 plus tax, $72.95 plus tax for kids 3–9).

BUSCH GARDENS One-day tickets cost $35.95 ($29.95 children 3–9). Senior citizens get 15% off, AAA members 10% off. Parking is $4 for cars, $5 for trucks or campers, $3 for motorcycles.
Hours: Daily 9:30–6, longer during peak periods.
More Information: Busch Gardens, Box 9158, Tampa 33674, tel. 813/987–5283.

SEA WORLD One-day tickets cost $39.95 ($32.80 for children 3–9), including tax. AAA members get a 10% discount. Parking is $5 per car, $7 per RV or camper.
Hours: Daily 9–7, as late as 10 during peak periods.
More Information: Sea World, 7007 Sea Harbor Dr., Orlando 32821, tel. 407/351–3600.

UNIVERSAL STUDIOS Tickets cost $37 for one day, $55 for two days ($30 and $44, respectively, for children 3–9), plus tax. They're available in advance by mail through TicketMaster (tel. 800/745–5000). Get them at the Orlando/Orange County Convention and Visitors Bureau ticket office at the Mercado International Market (8445 International Dr.) and you'll save about $4 per ticket ($3 for children). Or save $2.50 at the gate by using the free Orlando Magicard (available through the offer in this book or at the Mercado). AAA members get 10% off. Parking is $5 for cars, $7 for campers ($11 for valet parking).

Hours: Daily 9–7, as late as 10 during peak periods.

More Information: Universal Studios, 1000 Universal Studios Plaza, Orlando 32819-7610, tel. 407/363–8000.

WALT DISNEY WORLD Here, we're talking about the major parks (**Magic Kingdom, Epcot,** and **Disney–MGM Studios**), the water parks (**Typhoon Lagoon, Blizzard Beach,** and **River Country**), and **Discovery Island.** Single-day *tickets* admit you to just one of the major parks at a time, multiday *passes* to more than one. At press time, four-day passes are good for the major parks; the five-day pass and so called Length of Stay Passes (available to Disney resort guests and good from the time of arrival until midnight of the departure day) also cover the water parks and Discovery Island. Prices, which change regularly and include 6% tax, are as follows, with prices for kids 9 and under in parentheses: one-day ticket $40.81 ($32.86); Four-Day Value Pass $136.74 ($109.18); Four-Day Park Hopper $152.64 ($121.90); Five-Day World Hopper $207.76 ($166.42); River Country $16.91 ($13.25); Discovery Island $12.67 ($6.89); combined River Country/Discovery Island $21.15 ($15.37); Blizzard Beach and Typhoon Lagoon $26.45 ($20.67); Pleasure Island $19.03 for all. *See* pages 13–15 for more on tickets and passes.

Tickets and passes can be purchased at the theme parks, at on-site resorts (registered guests only), and at the WDW kiosk in Orlando International Airport. AAA offices sell discounted admissions. To park in the theme parks you'll pay $5 ($6 for RVs and campers; free to Walt Disney World resort guests with ID and at Typhoon Lagoon, River Country, and Blizzard Beach). Save your receipt; if you visit another park on the same day, you won't have to pay twice to park.

Hours: Hours vary but are longest during peak periods, when the Magic Kingdom may stay open until midnight or later. Note that although the Magic Kingdom, Disney–MGM, and Epcot's Future World officially open at 9 (World Showcase opens at 11), visitors may enter at 8:30, even 8. If you stay at a Disney-owned hotel, you can enter earlier. Discovery Island, River Country, Typhoon Lagoon, and Blizzard Beach operate daily 10–5 (during summer until 7 or occasionally 10).

More Information: For **general matters,** contact Guest Relations or Guest Services in any Disney theme park or hotel (tel. 407/824–4321) or the central WDW switchboard (tel. 407/824–2222). For **accommodations** and **shows,** call WDW Central Reservations (tel. 407/W–DISNEY).

notes

notes

notes

Fodor's Travel Publications

Available at bookstores everywhere, or call 1–800–533–6478, 24 hours a day.

Gold Guides

U.S.

Alaska

Arizona

Boston

California

Cape Cod, Martha's
Vineyard, Nantucket

The Carolinas & the
Georgia Coast

Chicago

Colorado

Florida

Hawai'i

Las Vegas, Reno,
Tahoe

Los Angeles

Maine, Vermont,
New Hampshire

Maui & Lāna'i

Miami & the Keys

New England

New Orleans

New York City

Pacific North Coast

Philadelphia & the
Pennsylvania Dutch
Country

The Rockies

San Diego

San Francisco

Santa Fe, Taos,
Albuquerque

Seattle & Vancouver

The South

U.S. & British Virgin
Islands

USA

Virginia & Maryland

Washington, D.C.

Foreign

Australia

Austria

The Bahamas

Belize & Guatemala

Bermuda

Canada

Cancún, Cozumel,
Yucatán Peninsula

Caribbean

China

Costa Rica

Cuba

The Czech Republic
& Slovakia

Eastern &
Central Europe

Europe

Florence, Tuscany
& Umbria

France

Germany

Great Britain

Greece

Hong Kong

India

Ireland

Israel

Italy

Japan

London

Madrid & Barcelona

Mexico

Montréal &
Québec City

Moscow, St.
Petersburg, Kiev

The Netherlands,
Belgium &
Luxembourg

New Zealand

Norway

Nova Scotia, New
Brunswick, Prince
Edward Island

Paris

Portugal

Provence &
the Riviera

Scandinavia

Scotland

Singapore

South Africa

South America

Southeast Asia

Spain

Sweden

Switzerland

Thailand

Tokyo

Toronto

Turkey

Vienna & the
Danube

Fodor's Special-Interest Guides

Caribbean Ports
of Call

The Complete Guide
to America's
National Parks

Family Adventures

Fodor's Gay Guide
to the USA

Halliday's New
England Food
Explorer

Halliday's New
Orleans Food
Explorer

Healthy Escapes

Kodak Guide to
Shooting Great
Travel Pictures

Net Travel

Nights to Imagine

Rock & Roll Traveler
USA

Sunday in New York

Sunday in
San Francisco

Walt Disney World
for Adults

Walt Disney World,
Universal Studios
and Orlando

Where Should We
Take the Kids?
California

Where Should We
Take the Kids?
Northeast

Worldwide Cruises
and Ports of Call